Les **Paul**
Bo **Diddley**
Duane **Eddy**
B.B. **King**
Chuck **Berry**
John Lee **Hooker**
Muddy **Waters**
Michael **Bloomfield**
Jerry **Garcia**
Peter **Green**
Carlos **Santana**
Jorma **Kaukonen**
Ron **Wood**
David **Gilmour**
Eric **Clapton**
George **Harrison**
Duane **Allman**
Jeff **Beck**
Jimi **Hendrix**
Jimmy **Page**
Keith **Richards**
Pete **Townshend**
Ritchie **Blackmore**
Angus **Young**
Brian **May**
Tony **Iommi**
Mick **Ronson**
Ry **Cooder**
Frank **Zappa**
Gary **Moore**
Joe **Perry**
Neil **Young**
Robert **Fripp**

The Stories of Six-String Myths and Legends

Masters
Of
Rock
Guitar

WHITE STAR PUBLISHERS

project editor / Valeria Manferto De Fabianis

editorial coordination / Laura Accomazzo

graphic design / Clara Zanotti

TEXT
Ernesto Assante

FOREWORD
Joe Satriani

PREFACE
Adrian Belew

> # The rock guitar master is a God of sorts, at least in his, or her, own mind.

That's what it takes to get the mojo up and running, to go out and stand in front of thousands of people every night, leading a revolution with a few power chords and some cool pants.

The true master of guitar doesn't get hung up on controversies such as technique versus feeling. They transcend them. They have to, because it's not easy being great. It's hard to be original and influential with flash and style. It's not child's play to write a great heavy riff or lay down an emotional, fiery solo to inspire millions. A true master creates their path and welcomes you to come along for the ride.

The guitar is a formidable lover and beast. It needs to be tamed and, at times whipped up into a wild frenzy. Playing the guitar onstage is an art form that puts sound and rhythm, harmony and melody, seriousness and irreverence together with attitude, tone and posture. The rock guitarist invites chaos and order in equal measure, in search of the perfect musical statement.

The exhilaration of performing onstage in front of an audience that's hanging on to your every chord, your every note, is one of the greatest things one could ever experience. This stunning book shows the Masters of Guitar in all their glory, caught up in the moment, making rock and roll dreams out of wire and wood. The images capture the guitarist wielding their mojo in a state of rock and roll grace.

Joe Satriani
San Francisco, 2009

What is it about the electric guitar that so fascinates?

What began as a plank of wood on someone's workbench has transformed into
THE ICON of rock music and the most popular instrument on the planet.
the electric guitar has many features to recommend.
PORTABILITY - Hard to imagine lugging a baby grand back to your hotel room each night,
but you can carry the guitar in a back pack.
SIMPLICITY - Your basic electric guitar has perhaps two knobs and one hole to plug into;
pretty straightforward. it's fairly easy to learn. but hard to master.
VERSATILITY - a player can do just about anything with the electric guitar these days.
When I began playing if you had a fender amp and a fuzzbox-you were hot!
Today I can play my guitar through my laptop. there is a billion $$$ industry
of after market accoutrements. everything from amplifiers and synthesizers
to picks and string winders.
LONGEVITY - when les or chuck or scotty first appeared who knew it would go this far.
but a funny thing happened: rock music never went away!
sound. It can range from raucus to sweetness. It can squeal or cry.
VOLUME - no question about it, the rock guitar is not shy.
as a communication device it's hard to ignore. it can blow a horn section right off the stage.
BEAUTY - the sensual form of the guitar's body has long been noted. it's sexy.
in the hands of a premier luthier the wood becomes a modern sculpture,
as seductive as a sports car at a fraction of the price.
IT'S FASHIONABLE - true, it can make you a rebel or a preacher,
but I believe the fashionable bit soon wears thin. There has to be something more.
PERSONALITY? now we're getting closer. players and manufacturers
have done just about everything to personalize the electric guitar.
We've added strings, pulled out frets, sawed off the headstock,
and cut the body into a myriad of shapes, sizes, and colors.
There was one guy who even burned his onstage! Anything to express your inner self.
And that's it! the one thing that sets the electric guitar apart is its capacity for **SELF-EXPRESSION**.
There is simply nothing like feeling your fingers bending a note and hearing the guitar sing.
Through self-expression comes passion. through passion comes perserverance.
Through perserverance you get to be one of the players on these pages.

So let's celebrate the electric guitar and the players who have made it unique.

Adrian Belew
february, 2009

Contents

One can have fun imagining the future,
dreaming about how the world will turn out.
It is also fun to try to fantasize about the past
and how the present might be
if certain events in the past had never really occurred,
if certain objects that are now integral parts of our lives
had never been invented.

> For example,
try to imagine
a world
without guitars.
No blues,
no flamenco,
no rock.

No blues, no flamenco, no rock. And in many parts of the world, no popular music—generations of musicians as well as legions of amateurs simply wiped out.

No more songs sung in front of a bonfire on a beach or under the window of one's beloved. This is by no means an exaggeration: without the guitar today's music would not exist. Would the world be a worse place? Perhaps. Certainly it would be different, because the importance of the guitar in the evolution of popular culture has been enormous, and the central role of the guitar in the development of music, especially the popular variety, is undisputable, and it has had and continues to have a place in classical music as well. It was also the protagonist of extraordinary moments in the history of jazz, the queen of country music and blues, and in its electric form it was the cornerstone of rock and roll. It is an extremely versatile instrument, suitable for a variety of musical genres and, above all, it is a complete instrument, an orchestra-instrument, so to speak, which offers the musician total creative and instrumental autonomy. This is the fundamental factor, together with its portability, that has made the guitar the most popular instrument in the world, entrusted with memories, emotions, and stories, both personal and collective, to be related and handed down. The guitar is the comrade that never leaves you by yourself and allows you to sing and play at the same time, to have both accompaniment and melody. The piano offers the same possibilities, but it has two, often insurmountable drawbacks: cost and limited portability. A guitar can be relatively cheap to buy, and when in the 1960s low-cost, mass-produced guitars came onto the market there was a boom in music that was absolutely unprecedented. We could go so far as to say that popular, mass-consumption music came into its own with the arrival of cheap guitars, the first mass-produced instrument that does not require special technical ability or an in-depth knowledge of music.

There is no official date regarding the birth of the guitar, but here we are discussing modern music and we want to try to narrate the story of a revolution, the one this instrument triggered in the world of music not once, but twice. The first time was at the beginning of the 20th century, when it became *the* instrument of popular music. This was a revolution that was not only musical, but cultural as well, and its impact was much more profound and meaningful than meets the eye (or ear). Then there is the myth and legend of the electric guitar. An extraordinary instrument that has been the expressive medium for young people throughout the world and which became a magical key that opened up their perceptions, their creativity, and their very lives. It is true to say that the rock guitar is a phenomenal musical instrument that has had many incarnations from the 1940s to the present, and and its sound continues to astound the entire world.

First of all, let us go back a bit and try to understand what exactly is a guitar. The following is a simple definition: "The guitar is a stringed instrument that is plucked with the fingertips or strummed with the fingernails or a plectrum (or pick). The sound is generated by the vibration of the strings, which are situated over the soundboard, which in turn rests on the sound box, which amplifies the sound. The strings are stretched between the tuning pegs, which are fitted onto the headstock by means of the nut, and the capotasto or bridge. On the neck, the fingerboard or fretboard is used to shorten the length of the vibrating string in order to attain the desired pitch (or notes)."

Thus, acoustic guitars are basically made up of two parts: the sound box or hollow body, which serves to capture and amplify the sound produced by the vibration of the strings, and the neck, which has the function of supporting the strings, regulating their tension and tuning, and obviously of allowing the player to find the right pitch and play the notes by pressing the strings on the fretboard. Electric guitars have no sound box, but instead have a solid body, and so without amplification their sound is very weak. Electromagnetic pickups are devices placed under the strings that convert their vibrations into electrical signals that are thereby amplified in the form of sound.

There are two large "families" of guitars, acoustic and electric, which differ both in shape, weight, size, and in the amplification, which depends on their shape. In general, acoustic guitars have a hollow body, which constitutes the sound box, while the electric ones have a solid body and need an electric amplifier in order to be played. Acoustic guitars can be divided into two types, classic and folk, depending on the strings used. Nylon is used for classical guitars and metal for folk guitars, which also have a larger sound box than their classical cousins and a neck that is reinforced with an iron truss used to counterbalance any changes in the tension of the strings.

Spain is the homeland of the classical guitar we all know. It developed from the *vihuela,* an instrument similar in shape to the guitar that was used to replace the lute. From the 16th to the 19th century many innovations were made to the structure of the guitar. At first the instrument was rather small, with four double strings. During the Renaissance, it was no more than 15 inches (40 cm) long, while a hundred years later its size had already doubled and a fifth pair of strings was added. The guitar, with the shape and size as we know it today, and with six single strings, developed only at the end of the 18th century. Also, it did not become particularly widespread until the 18th century, mostly because there was another stringed instrument that was similar and very popular – its "rival" the lute. The guitar we use now is the Spanish type with six strings. However, it is not the only option, because there are others with four, seven, eight, ten, and twelve strings. Guitars like these were used in the 1940s by jazz musicians and have recently enjoyed a revival, especially in hard rock and metal rock musical circles, because one or two lower strings are added to the classical six. And then there are the spectacular guitars with more than one neck. The most widespread is the one with two necks, with six and twelve strings respectively, or two necks with six strings that are tuned differently, while the three-neck version is rarer.

In many respects the Spaniard Antonio de Torres may be considered the "father" of the modern guitar. In fact, he was the first person to make a version of the classical guitar that produced a high volume and a tonal response that guaranteed good quality in all registers. De Torres's work is now considered innovative and almost all the succeeding makers of the classical guitar based their work on his studies and standards, which turned it into an extremely flexible and reliable concert instrument. Besides De Torres, mention should also be made of Domingo Esteso, John Gilbert (one of the major classical guitar makers in the world), and Manuel Ramírez, who had the most famous guitar-making firm in Spain. Naturally, the flamenco guitar became widespread in Spain. It is the wood, either cypress or rosewood, that makes the flamenco guitar different from the classical one and gives it a darker color.

But this is not all. The structure of the flamenco guitar also differs. Its sound box is built with thinner wood, so making the instrument lighter and easier to handle. In some models there is a tab plate known as *golpeador* or pick guard in the lower part between the bridge and the sound hole, which makes this instrument easier to use in a percussive manner.

The world of acoustic guitars with steel strings, which is mostly based in the United States, is also quite fascinating and marvelous. Although based on European guitars, it was created in the United States in the 19th century. Steel strings began to be used in the late 19th century and in the early 20th they became the standard throughout the United States, mainly as a result of the development of popular music, blues, country, and jazz. The jazz guitar evolved in the U.S. around the end of the 19th century thanks to Orville Gibson, who first conceived of a guitar with steel strings that at times was rounded and had two sound chambers at the sides instead of the single, central one in order to create a different sound.

And so there are many combinations and variations in the design and construction of guitars, such as electrified guitars, electro-acoustic guitars, semi-acoustic guitars, and the latest innovation, the digital guitar, which is more like a synthesizer than the old "analog" guitars and is used by musicians who did not settle for the instrument "as it was" and who continued to try to obtain new sounds and timbre effects. The guitar, unlike almost all other musical instruments, is a continuous adaptable, adjustable "work in progress." This is not to say that other instruments have not been modified, manipulated, and transformed over the years, but most of the changes have been personal, transitory, and effected to meet the demands of a single musician, while the continuous evolution of the guitar has paved the way for "definitive" changes and developments that have become an integral and permanent part of its history.

Many figures have played their parts in this instrument's history. A number of craftsmen and designers have developed the modern guitar into an extremely flexible and versatile instrument that can be used in many different situations. The first major guitar maker of the modern age was Christian Frederick Martin. He was born in Germany in 1796 but emigrated to the United States in 1833, settling in New York, where he opened a business that made and sold musical instruments. Martin then moved to Pennsylvania, where he established C. F. Martin & Company, which in a short time became one of the most famous guitar manufacturers in the world. The first standard model, produced in 1838, was still influenced by the work of the German luthier Stauffer, in whose workshop the young Martin had served as an apprentice. But already in 1850 the acoustic guitar model exhibited the quality and originality of his work, which reached its height in 1903 with the O-45 model and the OM-28 orchestral model made in 1929.

Almeria, in Spain, was the birthplace of the above-mentioned Antonio de Torres (1817-92), the most important figure in the history of the modern classical guitar. He was an ingenious guitar maker who from 1840 produced in his Seville workshops history-making models that later inspired future generations of luthiers. Another leading figure was Vicente Arias (b. 1845), who belonged to a famous school of luthiers that included Manuel Ramírez. Arias developed instruments from the model created by De Torres from the late 1800s to the early 1900s, achieving extraordinary results.

Orville Gibson (1856-1918) was, as already mentioned, an American who was to become one of the central figures in the development of the guitar in the 20th century. He began making guitars in the late 19th century and established his company in 1894. As Richard Chapman wrote: "The Gibson models were greatly influenced by the methods used for the violin family", which induced him to make guitars with a curved bottom and soundboard.

At this point in our story the electric guitar arrives on the scene. In point of fact there is no real "first" electric guitar, and it is difficult to attribute the birth of this instrument to any one person. There were several who were working at the same time and in different parts of the world on this fascinating development, which simply needed only to be completed. Some of these people were technicians and engineers, others were luthiers, while many were guitarists. Why was this development so urgent? It was necessary to free guitarists from their role as purely rhythmical instrumentalists who played "side by side" with the drummer and double bass player, a role inherited from banjo players. In fact, in the early 1900s popular music was dominated by the wind instruments - saxophones, trumpets, trombones, and clarinets - that had developed a loud sound and thus became the soloists both in large orchestras and small combos. It was virtually impossible for guitarists to play solos that could be heard, so the rhythmic function of the instrument was the only logical one when they played in groups. The first and most obvious answer was to amplify the sound, which was fraught with problems, but by working with total commitment several people found the solutions.

The first one to revolutionize the world of the folk guitar from top to bottom was John Dopyera (1893-1988). He was born in Slovakia and emigrated with his father, a famous violin maker, to California. John opened his first workshop in Los Angeles in 1920, where he repaired and improved stringed instruments, especially banjos, for which he patented many technical improvements. It is said that in 1925 the musician and musical instrument inventor George Beauchamp arrived in Dopyera's shop and asked if he could produce a guitar with a much louder sound so that it could be heard together with the other instruments in an orchestra. Many people had tried to achieve this, some even by using megaphones, but the results were simply laughable. Dopyera set about the task and in a short time produced a guitar with an aluminum cone under the bridge, a resonator that worked on the basis of an amplification method similar to those adopted in loudspeakers. This guitar, the body of which was either made of wood or metal, had a sound three or four times louder than normal folk guitars. It became famous and was known as the resonator or resophonic guitar. Dopyera was assisted in his work by his brothers Rudy and Emil, and with the help of some investors he founded the National String Instrument Corporation, which immediately embarked on the manufacture of metal guitars. Dopyera and Beauchamp set up their new headquarters near the shop of an excellent artisan, Adolph Rickenbacher (1886-1976), who shortly afterward began to work for the company as an engineer. Relations between Beauchamp and John Dopyera had never been particularly good, and eventually John and his brothers left the National Corporation and founded a new company, Dobro (a combination of "Do" from Dopyera and "Bro" from Brothers), which soon also became the name of their instrument. However, the brothers kept an equity share in the National String Instrument Corp. and then took over control when Ted Kleinmeyer sold them his stocks. As a result, many employees were fired, first of all Beauchamp.

In the meantime, in Europe other instrument makers were designing new guitars and succeeded in taking giant steps forward in the development of this instrument in the first half of the 20th century. Two of the leading figures were Epaminonda Stathopoulos and Mario Maccaferri.

The son of Anastasios Stathopoulos, a Greek manufacturer of lutes and violins who moved to the United States in 1903, Epaminonda Stathopoulos began making banjos in 1924 and guitars in 1929 with his company Epiphone – the name of which derived from Epaminonda's nickname "Epi" and the Greek word "phone," or sound. The most famous Epiphone guitar is the one used by Paul McCartney when playing the song "Yesterday."

The Italian Mario Maccaferri, on the other hand, designed a totally new guitar in the early 1930s. This instrument had two distinctive features: the sound hole in the shape of the letter D and an internal resonator, which was designed to increase the volume and also to offer different tones to the different strings. In 1932 and 1933 these guitars, known as "Maccaferries," were sold in England by the French company Selmer, which continued to produce guitars based on Maccaferri's designs even after he had stopped working for this company. Django Reinhardt made the Selmer guitars famous in the late 1930s.

The next steps in the history of the modern guitar were made once again in the United States. As we have seen, George Beauchamp was unemployed after his collaboration with the National String Instrument Company ended. But he did not lose hope. On the contrary, like his colleagues, he had long thought about electric guitars and now, taking advantage of this unexpected "pause" in his work, he concentrated on learning more about electronics and pursuing some of his ideas. After months and months of experiments, surprises, and failure, Beauchamp finally managed to construct, with the help of Paul Barth and Harry Watson (the latter had worked with him at the National), the first true electric guitar, which was known as the "Frying Pan" because of its shape. It was certainly not a handsome instrument but it worked quite well and Beauchamp could not wait to begin production. He then contacted Adolph Rickenbacker and the two founded the Electro String Instrument Corporation, which began to manufacture the "Hawaiian" electric guitars that Beauchamp had designed, which were originally called Rickenbacher and then Rickenbacker. The "frying pans" were not really traditional guitars but lap steel guitars, that is to say, guitars with a special sound that are played by being held horizontally on one's lap. These were the first guitars that adopted the electromagnetic pickup, and they can be rightfully considered the first true electric guitars ever made. Only a year later the company produced the first electric guitars on an industrial scale. But Beauchamp and Rickenbacker's achievements arrived at a difficult moment. In 1931 the Great Depression was in full swing and few people had money to spend on guitars, especially if they were innovative and electric, so only a handful of musicians used them. Furthermore, Beauchamp had trouble patenting his invention, because the patent office did not know whether to place the "frying pan" in the category of musical instruments or in that of electric apparatus, and a category with both did not exist since electric musical instruments did not exist.

In any case, it was not long before an entire line of musical products was developed by Beauchamp and Rickenbacker (electric violins, cellos, violas, and mandolins, and they even produced a prototype of an electric piano), but they never achieved real success. In 1940 Beauchamp left the company and died shortly afterward. Rickenbacker, despite the fact that he did not have the same faith in electric guitars as his partner, continued production and the company manufactured steel guitars up to the 1950s, but already in the mid-1930s he had begun to make traditional guitars, both electric and acoustic. In 1953 he sold his share of the company to F.C. Hall, which ended the first phase of its activity. Hall concentrated with more determination on electric guitars, abandoning the "Hawaiian" ones, which were declining in the market. It was the rise of rock and roll and a new generation of musicians who wanted instruments suitable for this new genre that finally led to the success of Rickenbacker, especially with the Combo and Capri models developed by Paul Barth. In the 1950s and 1960s the Rickenbacker guitars were amazingly popular, especially after the arrival of the Beatles, who made some of their models famous, particularly the 325 Capri played by John Lennon and the 425 used by George Harrison.

The father of the Ovation guitar was Charles Kaman, who founded the Kaman Corporation and created this innovative instrument in the mid-1960s. The body of the Ovation guitar consists not only of wood but also of various composite materials that often provide unusual sounds. Kaman was an aeronautics and aerospace engineer and used his scientific knowledge to improve the quality of the instruments with synthetic fibers, proposing the production of his creations to the Martin company, which rejected his ideas. So Kaman set up his own company, Kaman Music, for which he also made the first electro-acoustic guitar.

However, the two people who made a truly decisive contribution to the development of the electric guitar were without a doubt Les Paul and Leo Fender (1909–91). Les Paul, universally acknowledged as the "father" of the electric guitar, was not only a technician but also a first-rate musician and a major figure in 20th-century music. A musician from a very early age, in the 1930s Les Paul's creative ideas went beyond the capabilities of his instrument. Unsatisfied with what the market offered, he began to design his own instrument, to modify his guitar, as so many others were doing in that period, in order to attain more volume and compete with the other instruments in both the orchestras and combos. Everything began to change radically in 1938 when he moved to New York and had a fruitful relationship with Epiphone. He and Epi Stathopoulos became good and trustworthy friends, so much so that the guitarist asked Stathopoulos if he could work on his instruments in the laboratory on Sundays. Epi agreed and Paul began his experiments. At the end of 1941 he succeeded in finishing "The Log," a solid-body guitar. Paul later stated that he had sawed the sound box of a jazz guitar lengthwise in half and placed a solid block of wood ten by ten inside, attaching the neck and two pickups to this pole. With the solid wood the feedback was reduced to a minimum. He carried out many other experiments, modifying the Gibson and Epiphone models, but everything came to an end in 1943 when Stathopoulos died and Paul could no longer proceed with his Sunday work, so he left New York.

Les Paul then moved to Los Angeles, where his career as a musician reached new and well-deserved heights, no longer in jazz but in pop. Yet he continued with his experiments on the guitar, and in 1946 he tested "The Log" at the Chicago Musical Instrument Co., which controlled the Gibson Guitar Corp., but its president Maurice Berlin was not particularly impressed by Paul's technological innovations and did not believe that the solid-body electric guitar had any chance of becoming a success. Gibson had been working on electric guitars for some time, and in the spring of 1935 the company asked guitarist Alvino Rey to work together with the engineers from the Lyon & Healy Co. in Chicago to produce a prototype of a pickup. Then Gibson began its in-house experiments in earnest thanks to the efforts of Walter Fuller, who managed to design the definitive prototype. It was in late 1935 that Gibson introduced the classic hexagonal pickup on an F-hole archtop guitar, the ES-150 (ES stands for "electric Spanish"). The first guitar of this kind was produced by the Gibson establishment in Kalamazoo, Michigan on May 20, 1936 and was an immediate success. This paved the way for the electric guitar and the experiments, theories, and developments arrived one after the other, especially in the immediate post-war period. Under the aggressive leadership of its president, Ted McCarty, in 1949 the Gibson Guitar Corp. came out with two new ideas: the ES-5 model, the first guitar with three pickups; and the ES-175, the first "cutaway" guitar that also had a sharp point. Then came the turn of the solid-body guitar. "We wanted an instrument with inlaid edges that would remind one of the first Orville Gibson instruments made in the late 19th century, and gilded finish that would mean having an exceptionally valuable instrument in your hand," Gibson stated. McCarty decided that the Gibson company should also produce solid-body guitars, as Fender was already doing, but without imitating its competitor. He called upon Les Paul, and the result was a guitar with a heavy sound box made of maple and mahogany wood that also had a slightly curved front, which was accentuated by a gilded finish. This guitar was called Goldtop and Les Paul became a truly legendary figure. "I signed a contract with Gibson by which I would receive five percent of the price of every guitar sold, but in my public appearances I had to play only with a Goldtop," Les Paul recalled. "The relationship with Gibson became very close and in the end we managed to produce the model named after me, Les Paul, in 1952." But at this point his success seemed to run out. In the 1950s he became enormously popular both with Mary Ford and as a soloist, but in the next decade the rise of beat music put him in the background. And then in 1962 the Gibson Guitar Corp. decided not to renew his contract. But this "black" period soon came to an end, because in the mid-1960s a new generation of electric guitarists appeared on the scene and they all used the Gibson Les Paul guitar. This was a true triumph, and in 1968 the working relationship between Paul and Gibson was again in full swing.

As well as Les Paul and Leo Fender, there are two other people who deserve to be mentioned: the technician Paul Bigsby (1899-1968) and Merle Travis (1917-1983), a musician who in 1946 built a guitar with a very thin body, an original design, and the first tremolo arm or vibrato tailpiece with six tuners and a spring loader, which allowed players to "bend" the notes or even chords. This was a major innovation. In fact, it was one of the elements that the great Leo Fender worked on to realize one of the most important electric guitar models.

Unlike Les Paul, Clarence Leonida Fender was not a musician. He was born August 10, 1909 in

California and had some music lessons during his youth, but it was the electronics field that fascinated him most. A self-taught, tireless, and eternally curious experimenter, Fender was the first to understand that there was a potential mass market for musical instruments and that there was a new generation, which had grown up with rock and roll, for which music had a different meaning compared to the preceding generations and they were in effect a totally new market.

In 1938, at Fullerton, Leo opened the "Fender's Radio Service," an electronics shop and laboratory in one, where he sold and repaired radios and electronic gadgets as well as musical instruments. Among the musicians who made use of his services was Doc Kauffman, who had worked for Rickenbacker Guitars, and they began to experiment with new types of guitars, founding the K & F Company in 1944. Two years later Fender founded the Fender Electric Instrument Company. After some years of intense work and a great deal of experimentation, in 1950 he produced the first solid-body electric guitar, the Esquire, which was based on Bigsby's and Travis's ideas. It was soon renamed the Broadcaster when Fender decided to place two electromagnetic pickups on the instrument. This guitar is now known as the Telecaster because the Gretsch company stated it was too much like the name of their line of drums, the Broadkaster. In 1954, Leo produced the most popular and iconic Fender instrument, and indeed the rock guitar *par excellence,* the Stratocaster, by utilizing many of the innovations derived from suggestions made by musicians and experts in that period. This guitar had three single coil pickups that increased the potential gamut of sounds and tonal combinations, while the double cutaway design made it much easier for players to reach the highest frets. Leo Fender sold his company to CBS in 1965.

Obviously, the history of the electric guitar does not end here, but the great number of variations on a theme in the following years are closely linked with the history and events of a particular type of music. This long and exciting story began in the 1950s with the birth of rock and roll and the young people involved, with the beginning of a "modern" era that profoundly changed the customs of Americans and, in general, of the entire world. In the mid-1950s the future seemed just around the corner, technology was an integral part of everyone's daily life, electricity was available everywhere and this meant that almost every family had household appliances. Everything became easier, more useful, and "modern" simply by plugging in these appliances. The battle for the conquest of space began, movie houses featured science-fiction films, novels described future societies and worlds, and totally new inventions such as television changed our approach to, and relationship with, the world. This was the extraordinarily innovative setting of the birth of the electric guitar, an instrument that produced sounds that had never before existed, that had an unusually loud volume that did not require much effort to produce, an instrument with a "futuristic" look, and an emphatic image. This was not only a musical instrument; it was a key that opened the doors of the future, allowed people to say what had never before been said, and to play wholly new music. It seemed that it could change the world. And so a special musician was born – the electric guitarist.

It must be admitted that these musicians are strange, exotic creatures. They became greater stars than the other instrumentalists before them, be they saxophonists, pianists, or trumpet players. From the time the first wave of rock and roll began to sow the seeds of rebellion and the counter-culture, the electric guitar was already well established, a peaceful but headstrong weapon against tradition and the establishment. First it attracted and stimulated refined jazz musicians and had added a touch of malicious swing to African-American rhythm, but it was with rock and roll that it began to become an integral and permanent part of the dreams and aspirations of the new generation. Certainly, Elvis was not a guitarist, Jerry Lee Lewis usually played the piano rather poorly, and Bill Haley was a double bass player, but the "sound" was already there, and in any case just the riffs of Chuck Berry and others would be enough to place the electric guitar on its gilded pedestal. It was a vibration, a mere vibration amplified by a pickup that seemed to be a tiny step forward, an expedient or technical device invented to enhance the otherwise delicate sound of the acoustic guitar in an orchestra. And yet that very simple invention generated an entirely new cultural landscape. More than electric, it was simply electrifying. When Les Paul and Leo Fender carried out their first experiments on using electricity with guitars, they certainly could never have imagined the avalanche they were triggering. An overflowing river of creativity that swelled even further at the dawn of the 1960s with the likes of the Beatles, The Who, Rolling Stones, the momentous impact of Bob Dylan, the hippy culture of California, the iconoclastic fury of Frank Zappa, and many others. The river became an immense flood at the end of the 1960s when the genius of Jimi Hendrix exploded onto the scene.

At this point the electric guitar was no longer just an instrument. It was an icon, a standard that fluttered over the dreams of an era, a magical antenna capable of picking up desires, dreams and visions and of translating them into music. In a certain sense the electric guitar was rock, it embodied its dark sound and vibrant soul. It was a dominating symbol with unheard-of power. It was the most sensational combination one could imagine between the spirit of the times and an instrument's sound. The guitarist was no longer only a musician, but a "guitar hero," a mythical, legendary figure capable of going where no instrumentalist had gone before and of experimenting with styles and sounds that created new dimensions for the guitar. Hendrix was able to describe an entire universe. In his hands the guitar became apocalyptic, global, boundless, an infernal orchestra. However, we must not lose sight of the Latin ecstasy of Santana or the elegant blues of Eric Clapton, which in their own way also expressed a dynamic monument to the power of rock.

The flood showed no signs of receding. Quite the contrary, it gathered pace with the brilliance of Jimmy Page and the divine heavy sound of Led Zeppelin, and with the rise of Pink Floyd. Page was a natural phenomenon, creating new riffs that were nothing more or less than earthquakes. While Pink Floyd understood in an objective, definitive manner that the sound of the electric guitar could become a celestial diapason used to tune the soul, so much so that it could become a cult. The solid-body guitar, first and foremost the Fender, almost became an object of worship, a fetish, and many people wanted only to touch it, own it, and strum it as best they could, if only to experience the joy of playing an E major chord as loudly as possible, at least once. Since that time everyone has had an electric guitar in his garage or cellar, and the incredible longevity of this instrument is eloquent proof of its incomparable fascination. Music has changed, it has become digitized, records are now cut at home, and first synthesizers and then samplers have revolutionized the basic procedure of production. But the importance of the electric guitar has not even been affected at all. At the beginning of the 21st century it is still here, dominating every rebirth of rock music worthy of this name. In fact, there is now a revival of the electric guitar, and the aesthetics of the electric sound are more vital than ever.

If we were to select the "national team" of immortal rock guitarists, we would find it hard to limit it to the usual "first-string" players, and even adding the same number of "second-stringers" would be a difficult task. The reason for this is that the guitar is the leading instrument, and has been since the beginning of rock and roll, and thus there are so many first-rate players. The list that follows therefore merely proposes an elite of electric guitar players, and it goes without saying that everyone's choice as the "king" would be Jimi Hendrix, the musician who made the guitar something much more than a "six-string instrument."

Hendrix was born in America but success came to him in England. He viewed the guitar as a complete, total instrument that could produce unexpected sounds and complex harmonies. He saw it as an instrument that could create vistas of unknown worlds, utilizing a language that, starting off from the blues, ended up embracing all music. His career was short and tempestuous and he made a limited number of very intense albums in a few years. The quality and quantity of the material he created in such a short time is simply incredible, material that was destined to be dramatically plundered and plagiarized after his death by unscrupulous producers and record companies. To this day some of his recordings are surprisingly modern, unparalleled in creativity, and no rock guitarist has succeeded in coming close to his lyricism, inventiveness, his capacity to communicate with the sounds and noises of his guitar.

A starkly different approach to the guitar is that of Eric Clapton's, known as "Slowhand" among his friends. Certainly, blues music is always the common starting point, but, unlike Hendrix, Clapton has never tried to wander off the beaten track, he has never tried to broaden the vocabulary of guitar playing. He has concentrated on the intensity of interpretation, on pure, polished sound, on the expressivity of solo performances that are never theatrical and are always extremely measured and precise. For years – and often even now – these two, Hendrix and Clapton, were and have been considered the peak of rock guitar playing.

Alongside them (and not "below" or "above", in a useless and senseless classification) one must place Jimmy Page (from The Yardbirds to Led Zeppelin), Pete Townshend of The Who, Richie Blackmore with his Deep Purple (now gloriously replaced by the young and extremely popular Steve Morse), Martin Barre of Jethro Tull, and the matchless Frank Zappa – just to mention the first greats who come to mind. And it is still a great pleasure to discover, remember, and listen to so many different ways of approaching and using the electric guitar, an instrument that is anything but monolithic, by no means old-fashioned, ready to be held lovingly once again in some secluded garage in the outskirts of any city in the world by a boy who, having plugged in his amplifier, knows he is holding an instrument that can change the world. Perhaps only for the three minutes of a boisterous rock song.

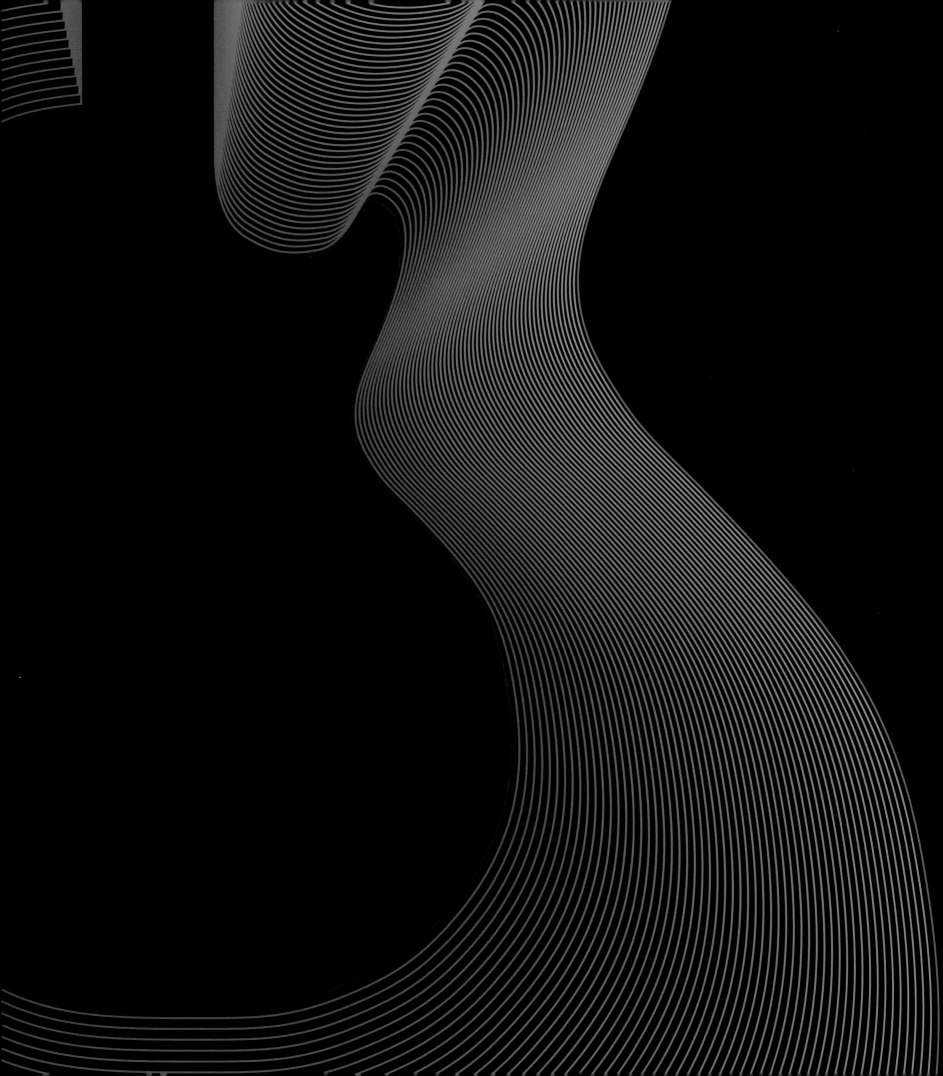

From the 1950s to the Present

< The 1952 Les Paul The Gibson Les Paul is the classic guitar created by Les Paul in 1952. To this day it is constructed using essentially the same materials and techniques.

< The 1950s During the period of his greatest success, the 1950s, Les Paul recorded albums with Mary Ford that reached top positions in the charts in both the United States and Europe.

> Lester William Polfus Les Paul (real name Lester William Polfus) at the beginning of his career. After playing the banjo he switched to the guitar, and in the late 1920s began to play with groups playing country music, after which he became passionate about jazz and then pop music. From the 1930s on he also concentrated on developing the electric guitar.

LES PAUL

Few people know that Lester William Polfuss is not only the legendary inventor of the Les Paul guitar for Gibson, but was also a great jazz guitarist (in the *Rolling Stone* classification he is listed as number 46, after Frank Zappa). A jazz musician is included by rights in a book like this one if he has contributed to the growth and transformation of rock music, and especially if he has also designed one of the great guitars.

Paul was born in Waukesha, Wisconsin and became interested in music when he was eight years old, first playing the harmonica, then the banjo and finally the guitar. Already at the age of 13 he was a semi-professional musician able to play good country music. When he was 17 he decided that music was his life, so he left school and became a member of the Wolverton Radio Band, where he discovered jazz music and began to make long tours. In the 1930s he lived in Chicago, where in 1936 he made his first recordings, two singles, one country and the other blues. In 1938 he moved to New York and founded his trio, which included Jim Atkins and Ernie Newton and with which he enjoyed his first major success. This led him to Hollywood in the early 1940s. He became so well known that in 1944

he was invited to play at the Jazz at the Philharmonic with Nat King Cole and then on the radio with Bing Crosby. Side by side with his career as a musician, Les Paul became increasingly dissatisfied with the electric guitars of the time, and so experimented with a prototype called The Log. In 1952 the Gibson Guitar Co. came out with the instrument that still bears his name, the solid-body Les Paul, the first guitar without a sound box.

In the meantime, in 1947, Paul consolidated his fame as an innovator with the first multi-track recording, "Lover," which had no fewer than eight different tracks for the guitar. In the late 1940s he reached the peak of his career, together with his wife, Mary Ford, using extraordinary recording techniques for such great hits as "How High the Moon," "Bye Bye Blues," "The World Is Waiting for the Sunrise," and "Vaya Con Dios." This success continued up to the 1960s, when Paul went into semi-retirement, returning to the recording studio every so often to cut an album. Twenty years later he was fully active on stage once again, and in 2006, at the age of 90, he won two Grammies for the album *Les Paul & Friends: American Made World Played.*

BO DIDDLEY

Almost all guitars have a round sound box, while the ones Bob Diddley used were all rectangular. This was as a result of a rather embarrassing experience the young Bo had that made him decide to make his own guitars so that they would be easier to handle and would allow him to jump around on stage without any risk of personal injury.

Bo Diddley was one of the least known legends of blues and then of rock, who rose to fame in the early 1950s and who became a legend and idol for the generation of those musicians, both British and American, who in the 1960s used the fundamental experience of the great bluesmen as a springboard to create the rock music that we know today.

Influenced by such greats as Muddy Waters and John Lee Hooker, Bo Diddley (a stage name that in the African-American slang of the Deep South means "nothing in particular" – he was born Ellas Otha Bates and changed his name to Ellas McDaniel) created a style and above all a type of rhythm that were unique. Drawing upon the rumba beat and other kinds of sounds, and then mixing them in with the repetition typical of classic blues, Diddley created a new genre of street music that, because of its special beat, could even do without complex harmony. Many of his songs consist of only one repeated chord. Examples of this are the hits "I'm a Man," "I'm Looking for a Woman," and "Who Do You Love?"

Diddley loved to experiment and his lyrics were very ironic. He immediately became known for his wholly unique style, both as concerns tuning and the sound he produced with his electric guitars, which were not yet distorted and dirty like those of Hendrix and the first hard rockers, nor were they "clean" like those of his predecessors because of his use of feedback, which was then taken up by the later generations of guitarists. Diddley's rectangular guitars were the first to be used for tremolo effects and particularly high tones, which extended the expressive potential of the instruments in ways that had never before been heard.

This great musician began to play and frequent musical circles in Chicago, first in churches and then in orchestras, and then he began playing in small blues bands. For many years, up to 1954, his favorite venue was Maxwell Street and then he managed to cut "I'm a Man" and "Bo Diddley," which reached number one in the R'n'B chart. This marked the beginning of his continuous success. From 1958 to 1963 he cut 11 albums for Checker Records, after which he took Europe by storm during a tour in 1963 with Little Richard. He became a hero for young rock musicians and fans. Over the years Diddley played with The Band, Rolling Stones, Clash, Grateful Dead, and many other bands. In 2005 he celebrated 50-year career side by side with Eric Clapton. Diddley died in 2008.

Custom Gretsch Rectangular
Gretsch Duo Jet

I got a tombstone hand and a graveyard mind,
I lived long enough and I ain't scared of dying.
Who do you love   (1956 - Who Do You Love)

< **Blues and rock 'n' roll** Bo Diddley was one of central figures in the development of American popular music. His style was a cross between blues and rock 'n' roll.

> **Still current** Diddley's music is still very much alive because he wrote a long string of standards that were especially influential on the rock generation of the 1970s, from the Rolling Stones to the California psychedelic bands.

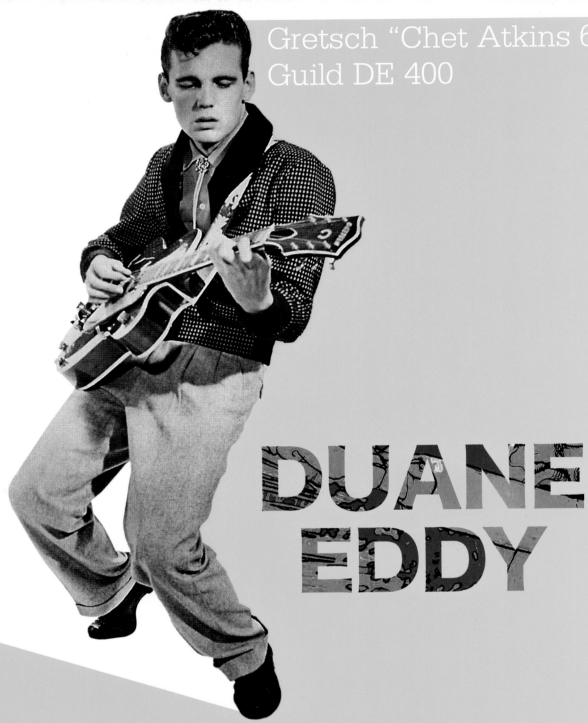

‹ › A pioneer of the electric guitar
Duane Eddy is not a major figure in the history of rock guitarists, but he was one of the pioneers of the electric guitar together with Chuck Berry. He cut the first single in the history of rock whose melodic line was played entirely on the guitar.

Gretsch "Chet Atkins 6120"
Guild DE 400

DUANE EDDY

Having to share with Chuck Berry the credit for familiarizing the general public with the electric guitar cannot have been an easy task. Especially as Berry was to enjoy a level of fame and glory that Duane Eddy never achieved. However, the original, true hero is Eddy, whose instrumental pieces were to influence generations of guitarists even beyond the field of rock'n'roll. Until 1958 the electric guitar was mainly used in a rhythmical role, with perhaps an occasional small and brief solo. In that year, though, Duane Eddy published "Moovin' and Groovin'", the first single ever to have the entire melodic line played by the electric guitar. No lyrics, no movements, just the sound of the electric guitar.

It was the first time this had happened and Duane Eddy rapidly became the first "guitar hero" in the history of rock. Eddy was also the inventor of the "twang" (an expression coined by producer Lee Hazelwood), a technique consisting of playing just the lower chord, in a standard key of E, while moving horizontally across the fingerboard. Eddy developed this technique probably just because of a habit acquired as a child, when he constructed his first guitar which was in fact nothing more than a wooden board with a single steel wire. The

possibilities offered by the "twang" are clearly limited, but the vast majority of riffs that are now part of rock history were derived precisely from an exploration of that single low chord. His staccato in "Peter Gunn" (a wonderful piece written by Henry Mancini and reinterpreted by Eddy as the theme tune for a television series) is accepted as perhaps the most famous ostinato in history – possibly even more appreciated than the one in "Smoke on the Water" – and is probably the first deliberate

phrase in music that one is taught to play when picking up a guitar for the first time. Four notes by four.

Eddy's work was extremely up to date in the 1950s and 1960s, but remained the same in the subsequent years and did not evolve. For this reason he was forgotten for a long period of time up until the beginning of the 1980s, when he published a self-titled album with the Art of Noise that included the umpteenth repeat of "Peter Gunn," which earned him a Grammy in 1986.

B·B· KING

Contrary to all the clichés about rock guitarists, who have reputations for leading lives marked by alcoholism, drug addiction, and decadence, and defying the common pigeonholing of blues musicians as long-suffering souls, B. B. King: the two "Bs" stand for Blues Boy, a nickname he picked up in the 1940s when he was a deejay) does not drink, does not smoke, is a vegetarian and is a licensed airplane pilot. The only "flaw" has been his long bout with diabetes, which however did not prevent him from celebrating his 80th birthday by standing and playing his guitar on stages all over the world.

Despite his apparently tranquil nature, B. B. King has been and is one of the most influential guitarists in the world of blues and rock, and *Rolling Stone* magazine has listed him as the third most important guitarist of all time, and the first among those still alive.

The blues king was born in Mississippi and was the nephew of heavyweight champion Sonny Liston. It is said that already at the age of ten he was no longer a virgin. During his childhood he fed on gospel and rhythm and blues music, and spent his time listening to jazz and spirituals, fascinated by such eminent figures as T-Bone Walker and Lonnie Johnson and by leading jazz guitarists such as Charlie Christian and Django Reinhardt, which helped him to gradually develop his unique style. In the late 1940s King began to pursue a successful musical career, when in Memphis he started making a series of recordings

(produced by the groundbreaking Sam Philips, who introduced and discovered so many musicians) that were broadcast on the radio and became great hits. This was the period when King decided to call his guitar "Lucille." It all started one evening in the town of Twist, Arkansas, in a rather seedy club, when two men got into a fight that caused a terrible fire. King ran outside like all the others, only to realize that he had left his beloved guitar inside. Risking his life, he raced into the club and saved his instrument. Later he found out that the row had been caused by a woman named Lucille, so he decided to give this name to his guitar, which he has used ever since, to remind him never to do such a dangerous thing again.

King's essential, singular and intimately blues style, consisting of "pulled" notes and a mixture of melodies he himself sings and

short melancholy improvisations, led him to success throughout the 1950s and 1960s with such hits as "Know I Love You," "Woke Up This Morning," "Please Love Me," and "When My Heart Beats like a Hammer." This success has lasted over the years, even without single hits (except for the legendary "The Thrill Is Gone," 1970), so that he has become world-famous and a favorite with the public as well as with great musicians (especially Eric Clapton). Proof of his popularity is the record he set by appearing no less than 74 times on the R&B Billboard Chart from 1951 to 1985, as well as the fact that he has performed live over 15,000 times during his 52-year career.

Gibson ES 335
Gibson "Lucille"

< **Memphis, 1948** B.B. King, one of the living legends of blues music, is portrayed in this beautiful photograph taken in the late 1940s, at the beginning of his amazing musical adventure.

> **Copenhagen, 1969** In this photo taken in 1969 in Copenhagen, B.B. King is playing the famous Lucille, the guitar he always plays (in many different versions) and is his legendary trademark.

< > **B.B. King and Lucille** August 6, 2005:
B.B. King playing at the Gibson Amphitheatre
in Universal City, California. On this occasion,
the great guitarist received a large birthday
card in the shape of a Gibson guitar for his
80th birthday, which was actually celebrated
on September 16.

> **Paris 1973** Chuck Berry, one of the
founding fathers of rock 'n' roll, while
performing at the Olympia, Paris in 1973.

CHUCK BERRY

"If you tried to give rock and roll another name, you might call it 'Chuck Berry'" John Lennon once said when describing Chuck Berry's influence on his generation of musicians. Berry was one of the founding fathers of rock and roll and with "Maybellene," recorded in 1955, established the "rules" of this genre. This was music that combined blues and old country music with topical themes that appealed to the young Americans in the affluent post-war period.

John Lennon was not the only musician to mention Chuck Berry as his main and direct source of inspiration, others include Eric Clapton, Keith Richards, Angus Young, The Who, Bob Dylan, and the Beach Boys. But Berry really led a double musical life, so to speak, since he himself admitted that he had learned to sing sentimental songs with good diction from Nat "King" Cole, while he would sing the blues in its simple, everyday language, much like Muddy Waters.

Chuck Berry's guitar sound was fundamental for the development of rock and roll. In fact, without a guitarist like him, this musical form would never have been the same, especially if we stop to consider that Elvis Presley and Bill Haley were basically singers and Jerry Lee Lewis and Little Richard pianists. Berry radically shifted the sound of rock and roll toward that of the electric guitar, elevating the riff to the level of an art.

For that matter, his relationship with his guitar was truly exclusive, so much so that in the 1970s he decided to make a series of tours only with his faithful Gibson guitar, without any other musicians to back him up, since he felt he could find bands every evening in the place he played in – a decision that led to several performances of questionable quality.

The fledgling Steve Miller and Bruce Springsteen also had the chance to play with Berry during these tours, and Springsteen himself recalls that at the time Berry did not even give them the sheet music, much less a list, of the pieces they were to play, since he expected the band to follow him after a short guitar intro.

Berry's rebellious nature meant that he ended up in prison three times (for robbery, pedophilia, and tax evasion), but this did not affect his fame and influence at all, and every time he came back stronger and more popular than ever.

The list of the songs he made famous is quite long, but mention should be made of "Roll over Beethoven," "Thirty Days," "You Can't Catch Me," "School Day," "Johnny B. Goode," "Rock and Roll Music," and "Sweet Little Sixteen," every one of which should be learned by heart if you want to grasp the essence of rock and roll.

< 1969 A fine portrait of Chuck Berry, the author of such classics as "Johnny B. Goode," "Maybelline," and "Roll over Beethoven," in 1969.

> Duck Walk At a 1980 concert held in Hollywood, Chuck Berry holds his Gibson guitar and executes his typical duck walk, much to the delight of his fans.

> Copenhagen, 1975 Chuck Berry dominates the stage during a 1975 concert held in Copenhagen.

Gibson ES 125
Gibson ES 355

JOHN LEE HOOKER

"I don't play flashy guitar, and I don't want to play like that. The type of guitar I want to play is angry, with angry blows of the pick." This is more or less how John Lee Hooker described his ideal of guitar sound, a musical style that inspired an entire generation of rock stars in the 1960s and 1970s. Indeed, his style made a great impact on the history of music thanks to its heavy, driving rhythm marked by the alternation of strong, droning bass notes played with the thumb and pick strokes on the upper strings at the end of every line for greater emphasis, a style that was already at its best in his very first hit, "Boogie Chillen'."

The story of John Lee Hooker belongs to another age. It is about a man who lived for 83 years and never learned to read or write, a man who ran away from home when 15 after having learned to play the guitar from his mother's second husband (who was a good blues guitarist). From then on the young John played his guitar while having to work as a laborer in Detroit auto factories up to 1948, when at the age of 29 he bought his first electric guitar and began to play in the clubs and in the street, where he was finally noticed and asked to record his songs.

Despite the fact that some of them became hits, Hooker continued to be exploited and cheated by unscrupulous producers and was paid a pittance. Thus, he recorded dozens of songs for different producers, using different pseudonyms (John Lee Booker, Johnny Hooker, John Cooker, The Boogie Man....) in order to make a decent living. His first success arrived in 1958, and then in 1962 he recorded one of the milestones of modern blues, "Boom Boom."

With time, however, Hooker's popularity increased greatly and his fans began to include young white people. Indeed, it was the young heroes of British blues that made Hooker into an idol, from Van Morrison's Them band to Clapton's Yardbirds, followed by the champions of the new American blues rock, first and foremost Canned Heat, who cut a record with Hooker in 1970.

Hooker's trademark was a loose, improvisatory style consisting of half-spoken songs, much like the Delta blues, and distinguished by very free rhythm. In fact, it was so free that he usually changed the tempi of his songs continuously without playing them twice in the same way. This is one of the reasons why his performance in the movie *The Blues Brothers* (in which John Belushi takes Hooker's sunglasses and beard) is the only one that was recorded entirely live. In the 1980s and 1990s he enjoyed great popularity, won a Grammy Award, and recorded albums with a great many rock stars, becoming an "old" guitar hero. But when all is said and done, Hooker always was a guitar hero, one of the legends of modern guitar playing, one of the fathers of the blues and of rock, a musician who cannot be ignored by anybody interested in becoming acquainted with the history of 20th-century popular music.

< **A guitar star** One of the legendary figures of American popular music as well as a father of the blues, John Lee Hooker is seen here wearing his trademark hat

> **An icon of rock music** John Lee Hooker is immortalized during a performance held in 1969, when the rock generation chose him as the inspiring spirit of rock's great performers.

MUDDY WATERS

McKinley Morganfield was born in Rolling Fork and raised in Clarksdale, Mississippi, where he was a fan of Son House. While observing the laborers working in the cotton plantations, he dreamed of becoming a musician. He was discovered by one of the greatest 20th-century musicologists, Alan Lomax, who recorded some of his pieces in 1941. But it was in 1943, when Waters moved to Chicago, that everything really began to click. Waters was the soul of modern Chicago blues, its electrifying and pulsating heart, the inspirer of entire generations of guitarists of both rock and blues. It is difficult, if not downright impossible, to imagine 20th-century blues without him.

In 1958 Muddy Waters toured England, showing people what the blues was for the first time to a public that until then was at best acquainted only with some folk-blues bands.

His series of revolutionary, but quite sober, perfomances introduced loud volume, the amplified electric guitar, and a thunderous beat to the British public, and the album that resulted from one of these evenings, *At Newport 1960*, converted an entire generation to his sound. That was the generation of Mick Jagger and Keith Richards, John Lennon and Paul McCartney, Eric Clapton and Jimmy Page, just to name a few. The 45-year-old Waters, who had grown up with the myth of Robert Johnson and had begun his professional career only at the age of 30, when his uncle gave him his first electric guitar, was astonished to discover that blues music was becoming more popular among Europeans than among his own fellow African Americans.

With his direct, sober blues, his highly personal sound and his profoundly black music, Muddy Waters changed the way to play blues for good. His singing style and the way he used the slide guitar made it very hard to imitate him or even follow him, and like many other musicians of his generation he could not play the same way twice.

When I play with my band on the stage I must be there with my guitar and try to bring all the sound onto myself," he once said to the magazine *Rolling Stone*. "And no sooner do I stop playing, the sound changes right away.

My blues seems very simple and easy to play, but it isn't. They say my blues is the most difficult to play in the world."

Despite this, after the "golden age" from 1950 to 1958, changing his band and his desire to seek new horizons diminished his fame and his inspiration to some degree, at least until the grand comeback he made in the 1970s accompanied by the same English musicians he had inspired. But times had changed, and this was a different Muddy Waters, a man who had given up playing the guitar and contented himself with singing, often songs that were not his.

< **McKinley Morganfield** Muddy Waters (whose real name was McKinley Morganfield) was born in 1915 and died in 1983. In this photograph from 1970 he is shown seated on a throne.

MICHAEL BLOOMFIELD

Highly regarded white bluesmen could be counted on the fingers of one hand at the beginning of the 1960s and Mike Bloomfield was one of them, and to this day he is considered to have been one of the true masters.

Discovered by John Hammond, the young Bloomfield – who idolized Muddy Waters and B.B. King – encountered great difficulties with the record company owners at the beginning of his career, since they were reluctant to trust a bluesman who wasn't black. This proved to be an obstacle to his achieving success, which arrived anyway in the second half of that decade after he joined the Paul Butterfield Blues Band and demonstrated his solo capabilities, and then when he participated in the recording of Dylan's "Like A Rolling Stone" after having performed with him at folk festivals.

Born in Chicago in 1943, Bloomfield became a blues fan when still quite young, and then played in the local nightclubs, where he met Paul Butterfield and Elvin Bishop, with whom he founded the Paul Butterfield Blues Band. This combo combined blues with psychedelic music and jazz, and became legendary mostly thanks to Bloomfield's long, creative solos, who not only excelled technically, but was also extraordinarily expressive.

Bloomfield was also a session guitarist, in particular with Bob Dylan, becoming a decisive factor in the electric revolution of this great songwriter and musician and working on Dylan's *Highway 61 Revisited*. In fact, he was so important that Dylan asked him to join his band, but Bloomfield refused, preferring to play the blues with the Butterfield Band. But then in 1967 he left the group and went to San Francisco, where he founded the Electric Flag band with the idea of playing "American music," which in his mind meant a fusion of blues, soul, country, rock, and folk. However, this experience proved to be short-lived. After cutting the first album Bloomfield abandoned this project and in 1968 formed the legendary Supersession band with Al Kooper, which was a true landmark in rock guitar playing. From 1969 to 1980 he was very active both as a soloist and cutting albums with other stars, but due to his addiction to heroin his style became less and less lively and interesting.

Yet Michael Bloomfield really did have something new to offer to music. Growing up as a harmonica player, he had the blues in his blood and even brought raga into his solos, which was a true innovation at that time. Improvisation played a significant role in his career, linking his playing style to that of some of the most sophisticated jazz players of the time. It is impossible not to take into account his stylistic contribution to the development of American rock, blues rock, and the psychedelic music of the 1960s.

This musician from Chicago also deserves the credit for reviving the reputation of the Gibson Les Paul guitar in the rock world at a time when it was being eclipsed by the Fender models. Bloomfield made the mistake of wasting his talent on indifferent albums during the 1970s and of literally throwing his life away, dying from an overdose in 1981, when he was only 38 years old.

JERRY GARCIA

Founder and leader of the Grateful Dead, Garcia's style of playing became the benchmark for the "psychedelic guitar." Less elaborate but far more incisive than a Cipollina, his inclination towards "singability" reflects his blues education and the American country influences for which he was certainly a spokesman (Garcia was also a remarkable banjoist). Like all psychedelic groups, the Grateful Dead were at their best when playing live and consequently the guitar player's charismatic personality and endurance during the long solos were of vital importance. Playing with or without his group, Garcia participated in over 2,000 concerts in the course of his life, which unfortunately ended far too soon.

It is possible to become an important guitarist even with an impairment that, for the average musician, would almost certainly mean professional death. At the age of four, little Jerry lost the middle finger of his right hand because of a tragic mistake made by his brother, who was chopping wood with an axe. Nevertheless, Garcia started playing the piano and then the guitar with great motivation and all without being taught. His technique, by the force of circumstances, required the use of a pick for both electric and acoustic guitars, but fingerpicking was also employed in some instances. His tendency to use long phrases made him particularly suited to the steel guitar, which he played on many occasions and even sometimes not with the Grateful Dead (his "Teach Your Children," with Crosby, Stills, Nash & Young is particularly famous). His highly original style combined bluegrass and blues with a melodic propensity that led him to become a guitarist who was more expressive than spectacular. Captain Trip, as he was called, was a true guru who, with the seemingly endless "Dark Star" by the Grateful Dead, defined the psychedelic manifesto of those years.

The list drafted by *Rolling Stone* magazine of the most important guitar players of all time, which has assumed an historic status and is clearly highly debatable, puts him in 13th place.

< > **Fame came in 1967** Peter Green, a talented and original British guitarist and one of the founders of Fleetwood Mac, is seen at left in a 1968 photograph and at right with his Gibson Les Paul during a concert held the same year.

PETER GREEN

Peter Greenbaum's name is indissolubly linked with that of Fleetwood Mac, but his great skill and power as a blues guitarist made him a point of reference for many musical developments. His fame came all of a sudden in 1967, when, after playing in Peter Barden's Looners, he replaced Clapton in John Mayall's Bluesbreakers. He was originally slated to replace Clapton for three months, but when the latter left the group he stayed on. This experience was short-lived, consisting of one album, the first-rate *A Hard Road,* which included two of his compositions. Once this experience was behind him he formed his own band, Fleetwood Mac, with Mick Fleetwood and John McVie, which was immediately successful. His sound was limpid and fast and proved to be a source of fascination for important musicians, such as Santana who decided to redo his "Black Magic Woman." This sound, so rich in harmonic tones, and echoes, was attributable to an "out of phase" magneto on his Gibson Les Paul guitar.

Bordering on what could be described as new age music, the track "Albatross" included three guitars and reached the top of the charts. But at that point Green, gripped by a religious crisis that was followed in the early 1970s by health problems, unexpectedly stopped playing. This was to become one of the longest and most unusual career interruptions in the history of rock music. He only returned to the scene some 20 years later, when he founded the Splinter Group, whose declared aim was to re-create as closely as possible the original sound of the blues. Due to his mental problems he often had to be hospitalized, and his playing was sporadic and elusive. In fact, in the 1980s Green ended up leading a tramp's life for six years. His brother took care of him and finally managed to get him back into shape. In the 1990s he made sporadic appearances on the stage and his recordings alternate magical moments with others marked by confusion.

Despite his career with Fleetwood Mac, his finest creation is probably the instrumental album, which he recorded entirely alone, entitled *The End Of The Game,* where blues and rock come together in a combination that he has never again equaled.

CARLOS SANTANA

Despite the fact that he is acknowledged as the king of Latin rock, Carlos Santana began his musical career in the mid-1960s playing blues, wishing to follow in the footsteps of his heroes B. B. King and John Lee Hooker. But the fertile atmosphere and creativity that dominated the San Francisco scene were so strong, and there were so many creative musicians to listen to, to meet, and play with, that a person like Carlos Santana could simply not be limited to only one genre.

The group Carlos played guitar in was originally called the Santana Blues Band, but only by chance, and he was certainly not its leader. However, it was actually a blues band that was very much influenced by the style of Muddy Waters. As it broadened its horizons and experience, the group began to experiment with innovations such as the inclusion of percussionists in the band, which greatly enthused the audiences at the live performances and above all created, together with the very electric orientation of Carlos, an absolutely unique sound characterized by counterpoint between the guitar and keyboard.

The road to success for the Santana band (which in the late 1970s got rid of the other two words, "Blues Band") opened up when the members met Bill Graham, who got them included in the Woodstock festival. Their performance in August 1969 was devastating, both due to the novelty of the repertory the band proposed and to the power of the rhythm section (sustained by the fiery drumming of the teenager Michael Shrieve), and not least the sound of Carlos Santana's guitar, of course. The execution of "Soul Sacrifice" that Michael Wadleigh included in the film of the concert was a major factor in the international fame of the band. Santana's guitar style differed radically from that of the other guitarists of the time, especially the leading stars of the moment, Eric Clapton and Jimi Hendrix. Santana used the distorter amplifier to produce long, sustained notes, "rolled" his pick without mixing notes in sequence, and combined typical blues phrasing with his propensity for Latin-American melody.

Abraxas is the album that marks the maximum blend of blues and Latin music, but Santana was intent on going further and pursued a musical evolution sustained by his growing interest in spirituality and jazz. Thus was born the record that marked a turning point, *Caravanserai,* in which the sharp and passionate sound of Santana's electric guitar was utilized for fusion experiments to create music that is Latin only in its base, but is actually a hybrid that, incredibly enough, is unique in the history of music and that paved the way for that art of contamination that often goes under the name of "world music."

Santana's guitar style is made up of a highly personal mixture of various influences that derive not only from other guitarists but also from other instrumentalists. Over the years his constant use of the wah-wah pedal, endlessly sustained notes, and distortion to bring out the higher notes, combined with a style that in its creation of melodies and solos merges strong rhythm and a very special taste for melody, have produced an absolutely unmistakable sound. Thus, Muddy Waters, John Lee Hooker, and B. B. King, who were the foundation of Santana's early style, were replaced by Miles Davis and John Coltrane as the guitarist's favorite influences, and this turn to jazz produced Love, *Devotion and Surrender,* which he recorded with John McLaughlin. It is a veritable hymn and tribute to the music of John Coltrane, a highly personal elaboration in a rock key of the great saxophonist's style.

At this point everything was ready for the "swan song" of Santana's most fertile phase, *Lotus,* which may be the peak of his career. The album was recorded live while he was in Japan on tour and was made with a carefully selected group of musicians. This two-disc album retraces and elaborates all of Santana's previous musical course, highlighting his new spirituality and experimentation with a powerful sound and at the same time with a sensitivity that are unique even for Santana. In the 1980s and 1990s Santana had many ups and downs until his sensational comeback at the beginning of the new millennium with albums and singles that were extremely popular. All of them were characterized by a fusion of pop, rock, and Latin music that is still unsurpassed in quality and fascination. This musician has no imitators. He has remained a singular guitarist without disciples but with great expressive power, an old "hippy" who can still move the public, even the youngest generation, with his guitar,

a "guitar hero" who is far from all kinds ❮ of excess and quite close to the heart of rhythm.

❮ **London 1993** Carlos Santana photographed in 1993 playing at the Capital Jazz Festival held in the Royal Festival Hall, London.

Following pages

❮ ❯ **An old young hippy** Two periods, two sounds, and two totally different looks: at right, Santana performing in 1970; at left, he is seen on stage in Mountain View in September 1997, in one of the performances that marked his great comeback in the late 1990s.

JORMA KAUKONEN

Jefferson Airplane was not just Grace Slick: "Slick personified the public image of Jefferson Airplane, drawing the interest and attention of the public and press alike. In fact, nothing was ever said or written about the band without the figure of Grace being in center stage." The guitarist Jorma Kaukonen arrived in San Francisco after a long stay in Pakistan. Before helping to found the legendary band, he accompanied the young Janis Joplin on the acoustic guitar. Joplin ("She was the greatest," Kaukonen recalled) was one of the progenitors of women rock singers, the other being Slick.

In 1965, the year the band was formed, Kaukonen began to play the electric guitar for the first time. He experimented with this instrument, producing a distorted sound without any sort of easily identifiable melodic line. This was an obvious indication of the psychedelic sonority he was beginning to develop, which was already effective and astounding. Kaukonen himself stated that Clapton's playing during the Cream period was the greatest influence on his own style. Indeed, the decisive transition from the folk rock of his early career to the sound of *Surrealistic Pillow* was due to the powerful effect created by the English trio.

However, the blues man's career did not end with Jefferson Airplane. In 1970 he founded the acoustic duo Hot Tuna with bass guitarist Jack Casady, which occupied all his energy from 1973 on, when the rock phase of his band could be considered over. The original Hot Tuna band included Marty Balin and Joey Covington, but the fulcrum of the group was Kaukonen and his guitar sound, which at first was acoustic and then, in 1972, became electric, often in a fantastic and imaginative dialog with the violinist Papa John Creach. In the 1970s the band became famous for its long jams and Kaukonen's interminable solos, which were never banal or boring, lying somewhere between blues and psychedelic music. However, the guitarist never abandoned his acoustic guitar, with which he cut many solo albums, the best known of which is *Quah* (1974), which included the unforgettable "Genesis," his trademark piece. In 1978 Hot Tuna broke up and 1979 saw the birth of Vital Parts, in which Kaukonen experimented with new wave music – without much success it must be said. Then he went back to the acoustic guitar and the Hot Tuna band, with whom he still plays.

> **New Barbarians** Ronnie Wood was the
third guitarist after Brian Jones and Mick
Taylor to flank Keith Richards in the Rolling
Stones. Here he is seen playing in 1979 with
New Barbarians, the band he formed with
Keith Richards during periods when the
Rolling Stones were not touring.

RON WOOD

Ron Wood is the least-known member of the Rolling Stones. He joined the group in 1976 as a replacement for Mick Taylor. His role is as an accompanist, occupying a purely complementary role to the guitar playing of the undisputed master of the group, Keith Richards.

Despite the fact that he has belonged to the band for over 30 of his 40 years of activity, Wood has never been satisfied with being just the sideman of the Rolling Stones and has continued to play with many other friends and musicians. Consequently, his guitar and his sober style have literally traversed the history of rock music like a red thread that connects and combines very distant and different experiences, personalities, and albums. A close friend of Rod Stewart – with whom he shared a seminal period in his musical career and then recorded a very successful unplugged concert for MTV, *Unplugged... and Seated* – Wood had begun with much more aggressive bands such as The Faces (a band that was later credited with inspiring such punk

revolution combos as the Sex Pistols) and continued as a sideman for Steve Winwood, Rick Grech, Pete Townshend, Jim Capaldi, and even Eric Clapton in the famous 1973 Rainbow Concert, which marked his return to the stage after his heroin rehab stint. Then came the Stones, and Wood's life changed completely. He became a giant rock star, light years away from his original lifestyle. The synergy between Wood and Keith Richards was magical and the two were a perfect combination: Keith with his riffs and Ronnie with his rhythm; the former an essential, if not actually elementary, soloist, the latter a decidedly more swingy and creative one. Wood let Richards have center stage and never tried to overshadow him, but he had all the room he needed to show that he, and not Brian Jones or Mick Taylor, was the true and ideal partner for Jagger & Richards.

There is also another very different aspect to Ronnie Wood's musical career that can be seen in his performances with Van Morrison, Bob Dylan, Joni Mitchell, and Neil Young in "The Last Waltz," The Band's farewell concert held in 1976 and immortalized in a documentary with the same title directed by Martin Scorsese. Here he is the eternal sideman, with a cigarette planted on one side of his mouth while playing blues. This is the perfect Ron Wood, less of a showman and more solid and lovable, a towering figure in the panorama of British rhythm guitarists, a musician who still has a lot to impart to the younger generations. And he does so through his solo albums, records in which he sings and composes, something he obviously cannot do with the Rolling Stones.

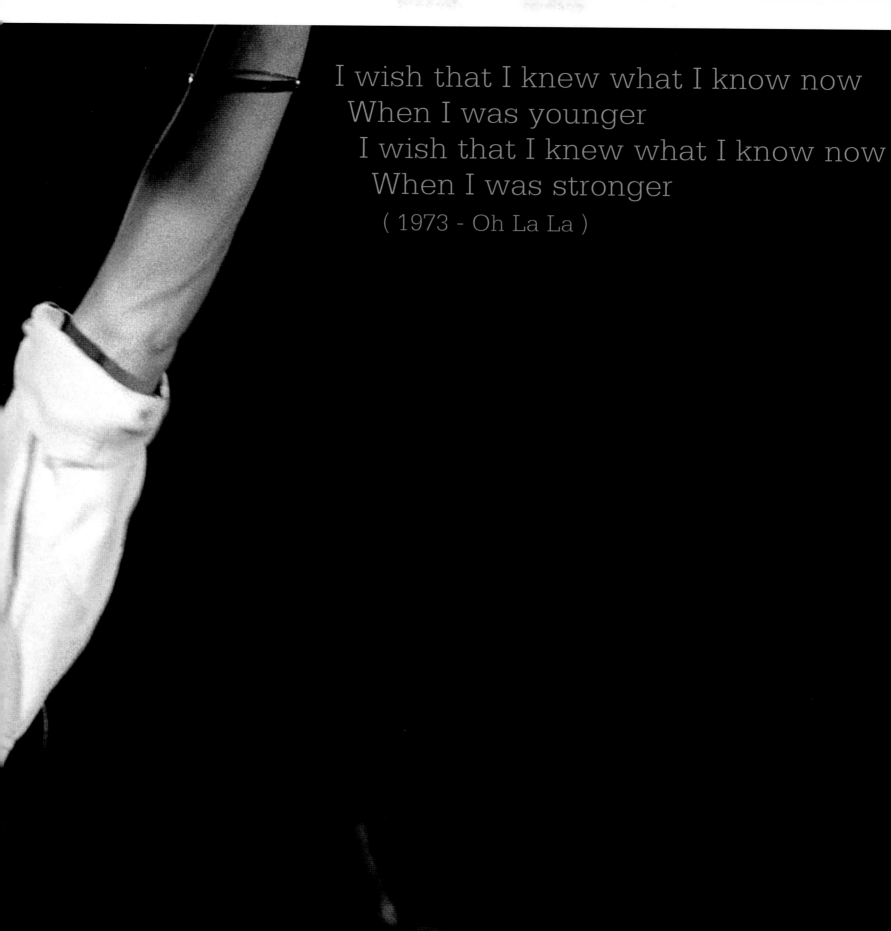

I wish that I knew what I know now
When I was younger
I wish that I knew what I know now
When I was stronger

(1973 - Oh La La)

<> **Toronto, 1979** Ronnie Wood arrived on the rock
scene with The Faces, the first-rate English band whose
vocalist was Rod Stewart. This photo was taken in 1979,
at the end of a concert held in Toronto, Canada.

Sunburst Fender Stratocaster
Fender Telecaster
Gibson Firebird

< On stage Wood is not only a guitarist but also a composer, vocalist, and a painter. In this photograph he is seen with Keith Richards.

> Boston, 2002 Every time the Rolling Stones release a new album they organize a sensational worldwide tour and take their greatest hits "on the road." Here Ronnie Wood is shown performing on the opening concert of the Licks Tour in Boston on September 3, 2002.

DAVID GILMOUR

No doubt about it, there is a vast difference between Syd Barrett and David Gilmour. It is also true that, beginning with *Ummagumma* (1969), Gilmour has provided Pink Floyd with a unique and very evocative sound and style, although it is less visionary than that of his co-founder friend, for whom Gilmour filled in at first. Actually, Syd learned to play better thanks to David, who taught him some basic Rolling Stones riffs, among other things. It was then that Barrett managed to create his highly personal sounds in so many other ways with his instrument.

Gilmour's style is highly original, and this is the reason why, with respect to the type of music that Waters has in mind, he can do without unbridled virtuosity. This taste for melody and his remarkable lyrical vein are the main features of his solos, which are very long and fluid.

It must be said that – at least in the golden age of Pink Floyd (up to *The Wall*, 1979) – Roger Waters never set any limits to Gilmour's imagination, taking in consideration his technical background, which made him more versatile. For that matter, the psychedelic approach that made this band famous required long, and often times very slow, expressive passages, in the quest for sound solutions in the entire development of a piece (an example in point is "Shine on You Crazy Diamond"). Gilmour is unmitigated pure expression, which is worlds apart from the virtuosity based on speed and volume. Yet at the same time he is a remarkable innovator in terms of sonority and the manipulation of guitar sound, especially in the first phase of the history of Pink Floyd. Gilmour himself calls his style a "mishmash" of different elements – blues numbers, passages from musicals, romantic songs, melodies he has heard and stored in his memory, together with all the solos he has listened to in his lifetime and has greatly admired: "Every time you hear someone else's melody, whatever kind of music it is, that melody occupies a space in your brain. And when you create your music you recall what you have inside yourself."

Gilmour was born in Cambridge in 1946 and became a good friend of Syd Barrett, whom he met at school and with whom he began to play music. He played with Joker's Wild, the Flower and Bullett before being asked to join Pink Floyd, of which Barrett was already a member. When Barrett's illness forced him to leave the band for good, Gilmour became the singer and sole guitarist, making a fundamental contribution to the development of the style and sound of this legendary British combo.

Recently, a classification was made of the best guitar solos of all times, and first place was given to David Gilmour for his "Comfortably Numb." Naturally, one can argue that this is not the only "number one," but there is no doubt that it is the best example of his guitar playing: evocative, vociferous, blinding. Perhaps this is why Pete Townshend called him one of the greatest guitarists on the planet.

< Pink Floyd The famous band is seen here with all its members: Nick Mason, David Gilmour, Roger Waters, and the late Rick Wright.

> Falkoner Centre, 1970 David Gilmour became a full-fledged member of Pink Floyd when Syd Barrett left the band. This photo of Gilmour with his Bill Lewis guitar was taken in 1970.

Fender Stratocaster

> **London, 2005** After years of rifts and legal disputes, Pink Floyd reunited for a single event at Live 8, at Hyde Park, on July 2, 2005.

(76/77)

ERIC CLAPTON

Eric Clapton is one of the central figures in the evolution of rock music in the second half of the 20th century. He has played a crucial and pivotal role in many developments and of various phases in the innovation of this musical language, and is one of a large group of guitarists who have led blues from its original form to modern rock. Clapton has for a long time been considered the greatest guitarist in the world, earning a huge following of faithful admirers.

His life has been marked by accidents, death, separation, and tormented love, and, like a true blues musician, he has had a pain-filled, tragic existence since his childhood.

He was raised by his grandmother and until he was nine he thought she was his mother and that his real mother was his elder sister. Clapton was one of the first people to discover the great talent of Jimi Hendrix, with whom he had a strong friendship that only ended with the latter's untimely death. He suffered terribly for the passionate and unrequited love he felt for Pattie Boyd (who later became his wife), who at the time was married to his close friend George Harrison; one of his sons died when only three; and while he was touring with fellow guitarist Stevie Ray Vaughan he let him have his seat on a helicopter that later crashed and killed Vaughan.

Side by side with this tormented life there has always been his music, a form of blues closely bound to the American origin of this genre and influenced most of all by such guitarists as B. B. King and Robert Johnson. This is a musical genre the reappraisal of which Clapton has contributed to with his main bands (Yardbirds, Cream, and Derek & The Dominoes), also continuously paying homage to it in his solo career, thus becoming (partly due to his fame) living proof of the vitality of blues and the deep bond it has with rock.

It is precisely his fame that has been one of the most important components of his career. Already in the mid-1960s, when, having left Yardbirds, he began a series of gigs in night clubs with the Bluesbreaker band, Eric Clapton enjoyed success far above the norm. This was clearly symbolized by a very famous graffito painted on the walls of the London underground, "Clapton Is God."

The discovery of the still unknown Jimi Hendrix made a tremendous impact on Clapton's life. When he heard Hemdrix play he told his friend George Harrison that he wanted to stop playing the guitar. But rather than quit, Clapton continued to gain even more success and fame (even more than Hendrix in that period), which culminated in the early 1970s with the album *Layla and Other Assorted Lovesongs*, which he cut with Derek & The Dominoes and which included "Layla," a song inspired by an Indian myth concerning unrequited love, a sort of allegory of his deep and hopeless infatuation with Pattie Boyd.

However, adversity continued to plague his existence and for a long period Clapton had to cope with drug addiction, which even forced him to sell many of his guitars. He sold both his Gibsons, which he had played for the entire 1960s, and the Fenders, which with time had become his very symbol, so much so that the Leo Fender company made its first custom-built guitar for him.

< **Live, 1990** The English guitarist Eric Clapton is enamored of the blues and his playing style has earned him the nickname "Slowhand."

> **London, 1996** Clapton is a sort of British institution. Here we see him during a concert held in Hyde Park in1996 for the Prince's Trust.

Like the way it gets me, every time it hits me
I've got a rock'n'roll, I've got a rock'n'roll heart   (1983 - Rock'n'Roll Heart)

< **The Netherlands, 1990** In the final phase of his career, Clapton made a sensational return to the blues, after enjoying such success in the 1980s and 1990s with a form of elegant and sophisticated pop. Today he is considered a great who inspires many guitarists of the younger generations, precisely because of his skill in adopting different styles and genres with such elegance.

Gibson Les Paul
Gibson ES 335
Fender Stratocaster

SLOW HAND

GEORGE HARRISON

One could almost say that George Harrison was Eric Clapton's younger brother, because the two were bound by a deep and lasting friendship and Harrison's guitar style is very similar (although quite inferior technically) to that of the former leader of Cream. Although technically not exceptional or gifted, one should not underestimate the impact George Harrison made on the history of rock music, because, above all with the Beatles, he inspired an entire generation to play the guitar, to pick up this instrument, compose songs, and experiment with solos. He created a sound that to this day is absolutely unmistakable, unique, inimitable. One might say that his

instrument is the beat guitar, which marked his beginnings in the 1960s and gradually became the guitar sound of pop music that is still loved by the public. However, Harrison's achievements go even beyond this, because he was also an extraordinary experimenter, a first-class composer, and a fundamental rhythm guitarist.

In short, George Harrison was a major figure in the music world not only because he was a member of the Beatles or because he was particularly original, but because he taught so many other musicians who followed him the art of synthesis, of the compelling but not aggressive solo that, while brief, outdoes the riff in articulation. "Here Comes The Sun" and "Something" have these features, and it is certainly no accident that his masterpiece, "While My Guitar Gently Weeps," includes a more complex solo played by Eric Clapton.

Starting with his activity with the Beatles, Harrison found some time to write songs, and as a guitarist he was a sophisticated arpeggio or broken chord player, one who did what Lennon, who was a rhythmical guitarist, did not do. He mainly used the pick in his phrasing, and whenever he had the opportunity (in the last albums with the Beatles and later in his work as a soloist) he developed a good and well-balanced slide technique. In fact, it was from the 1970s on, when he had more time to himself, that Harrison produced his most interesting creations. Two albums that everyone should have in their collection are *All Things Must Pass*, which includes the single "My Sweet Lord" (famous partly because it was accused of plagiarism), and *Concert For Bangladesh,* which is outstanding for its top performers: Dylan, Clapton, Ringo Starr, and Ravi Shankar, the most famous Indian

musician of the time and a close friend of Harrison. In this regard, it is worthwhile recalling that Harrison was the first person to introduce an instrument like the sitar into pop music, even though he actually utilized only its sound. For example, in "Norwegian Wood" there is no piece written specifically for the sitar, as this instrument only doubles the guitar theme. But the mere fact that he presented a new sound to an entire generation is enough to allow him to take his place among the greats.

Then again, he was a member of the most important band in the history of popular music, providing it with its characteristic sound – quite an achievement by anybody's standards.

I look at the world and I notice it's turning
While my guitar gently weeps
With every mistake we must surely be learning
Still my guitar gently weeps

(1968 - While My Guitar Gently Weeps)

< **Group photograph, 1963** The Beatles -
Paul McCartney, George Harrison, Ringo Starr,
and John Lennon - at the Alpha Television
Studios in Birmingham in 1963.

> **Beatlesmania** Beatles fans, true to the
hysterical passion of "Beatlemania," always
followed the band from one public
appearance to the other. Here we see
Harrison on a train while recording *A Hard
Day's Night* in 1964, with his worshipful fans
watching him.

< George the hippy Of the four Beatles, George Harrison was the one most involved in hippy culture, and even went so far as to take the band to India to meet and talk with the guru Maharishi Mahesh. He was also the first of the four to go to San Francisco during the 1967 Summer of Love, as is testified by this photo showing Harrison in Golden Gate Park after having roamed around the Haight-Ashbury neighborhood for an hour.

> George in 1970 The Beatles broke up officially in 1970, the year that Harrison released the triple album *All Things Must Pass*.

Following pages

< The Concert for Bangladesh The most famous event connected with George Harrison's career was the first major rock charity concert, the Concert for Bangladesh, which took place in Madison Square Garden on August 1, 1971.

> Traveling Wilburys Bob Dylan and George Harrison were great friends and together founded the Traveling Wilburys. Here they are photographed playing together for the Rock 'n' Roll Hall of Fame in 1988.

DUANE ALLMAN

It is difficult to say whether the second place in *Rolling Stone* magazine's list of the best guitarists of all time, right after Hendrix, was awarded to Duane Allman as a true testimony to his talent or merely as a sentimental gift to someone who became a myth too early in his life. Tragically, Duane was only 25 years old when he died in a motorcycle accident in 1971, but even so he, together with his brother Gregg, had already made a permanent mark in the history of rock with the Allman Brothers Band, especially with the album recorded live (Duane's last one), *At Fillmore East.*

Allman was one of the first rock guitarists who really explored the depths of the potential of the instrument. Thus, in a very short time he became one of the leading exponents of the "slide" technique and in the use of open E tuning (E, B, E, G, B, E), which made it possible for him to create fascinating improvisations. This was an expedient similar to the one used in jazz with the modal tuning procedure.

The two-guitar harmonies created with the great guitarist Dicky Betts, the prefect partner for Allman in his long passages, benefited from their deep knowledge of the instrument and consisted of a simple melodic counterpoint.

Even the purely manual approach was different from the usual one utilized by rock guitarists of the time. Allman almost never used the pick, preferring his thumb, forefinger, and middle finger. This was certainly a nonconformist technique, so much so that it made many classical and electric guitarists turn up their noses because it seemed very limiting. In reality this technique allowed Allman to concentrate so much on his touch that he was able to create a wide range of sounds that would have been very difficult, if not impossible, to reproduce with the pick. Later, even Mark Knopfler chose to adopt this fingerpicking method.

It must be said that the music and musicians that influenced Duane were also quite different, ranging from Chuck Berry to Jeff Beck, with the Beatles, Rolling Stones, Miles Davis, and John Coltrane in between. That is to say, with his solos Allman interpreted the quintessence of the language of rock music, drawing from various musical elements, which he then transformed into something totally different. Furthermore, he was a passionate and fascinating soloist who used his fantastic technique solely to create emotions, not useless display. Allman also involuntarily publicized a brand of cold and cough medicine, Coricidin, when he used an empty bottle to play the slide technique.

> **Los Angeles, 1977** Jeff Beck, the prince
of British blues guitarists, during a 1977
concert held in Los Angeles.

JEFF BECK

In a hypothetical classification of the greatest guitarists in the history of rock, Jeff Beck would surely be ranked among the first ten. His extraordinary technique is coupled with equally outstanding creativity and by a style that over the years has become a marvelous amalgamation of blues, jazz, and rock. The eclectic, experimental, and very temperamental Beck has succeeded in remaining at the top of his profession and has continued to collaborate with some of his more famous colleagues, though he has never achieved the fame commensurate with his talent and his recording output has been episodic, to say the least.

His career began as an uphill struggle when around 1966 he was asked to replace Eric Clapton in the "national team of English rock blues guitarists," Yardbirds, where he flanked Jimmy Page for a certain period. After that experience he began his solo career with the Jeff Beck Group, playing lead guitar, in which he followed the path of rock music, accompanied by such fine musicians as Ron Wood and Rod Stewart, who left the band in 1970 to play with Faces. With Wood and Stewart he made two albums, *Truth* in 1968 and *Beck-Ola* the following year, which are generally acknowledged as essential albums in the development of hard rock in that period.

The next step was to found a super band with two musicians from Vanilla Fudge, Tim Bogert and Carmine Appice, but an automobile accident prevented Beck from playing for a time and in 1971 he formed a new version of the Jeff Beck Group to record two albums that were received very well. Appice and Bogert finally teamed up with Beck in 1973, but by then times had changed and Beck himself did not seem to be so sure of himself.

With his eccentricity, strong temper, and continual changes of mind, Beck ended up making all his colleagues go crazy, even George Martin, the famous producer of the Beatles. When the two worked together in 1975 on *Blow By Blow*, the record that marked Beck's comeback on the music scene, Beck was never completely satisfied with his solos and with the overall sound, and usually a few days after every recording session he would call Martin and ask him to make a new recording. He even went so far as to call Martin months after a recording in order to set things right, only to hear the latter reply: "Sorry, Jeff, but the record is in the shops!"

Despite the disbanding of the Jeff Beck Group, Beck has continued to play with Clapton, Sting, Vinnie Colaiuta, Jan Hammer, John Paul Jones, Roger Waters, Brian May, and Steve Ray Vaughan, and still opens many of B. B. King's concerts. In fact, despite his lack of constancy the quality of his music has always been greatly appreciated, especially among fellow guitarists and critics, who have awarded him several Grammies.

Yardbirds

I'd give you everything and more, and that's for sure / For your love.
I'd bring you diamond rings and things right to your door / For your love.
(1965 - For Your Love)

< **British Blues** The Yardbirds were among the first famous bands
that played so-called British blues. In this photograph we see Jim
McCarty, Jeff Beck, Keith Relf, Paul Samwell-Smith, and Chris Dreja.

> **Geoffrey Arnold** Jeff Beck, whose real name is Geoffrey Arnold,
played with The Yardbirds after Eric Clapton left the group.

Fender Esquire
Fender Stratocaster
Gibson Les Paul

< **The Jeff Beck Group** Jeff Beck in action at the Fillmore West venue in San Francisco, in 1968. At that time the Jeff Beck Group included Ron Wood and Rod Stewart.

> **The Yardbirds** An almost obsessive perfectionist, Beck is totally concentrated during this live performance.

Following pages

< > **Two maestros of white blues** The Englishman Jeff Beck and the American Stevie Ray Vaughan are immortalized in this 1980 photo. Despite the fact that he is one of the greats of the first generation of British blues, Beck did not attain the success enjoyed by his contemporaries, Eric Clapton and Jimmy Page. Vaughan, on the other hand, became a star just at the time when the guitar seemed to have gone out of fashion and the electronic keyboard came to the fore.

JIMI HENDRIX

One thing is certain, James Marshall Hendrix was the most important guitarist in the history of rock music. By innovating the style and technique of guitar playing, and by modifying the role this instrument played in rock bands, he was a major influence in making the guitar *the* instrument of rock music. This alone is enough for Hendrix to take his place in any encyclopedia of 20th-century music. But he was not only this. It is difficult, if not downright impossible, to describe the Hendrix sound with words, the impact made by his live performances, the sheer power of his sound, the unpredictable nature of his solos, and the profundity of his expression. It is an awesome task to describe the greatness of such a musician with the space available here. Hendrix was the embodiment of the youthful counter-culture that was developing when rock took center stage. His sound surpassed the usual confines and sparked a spectacular new relationship between the spirit of the age

and politics, with the quest for personal enlightenment and aspiration.

The young Jimi was a guitarist with African American, Native American, and white blood in his veins who began his musical career in rhythm and blues and formed his own band, which played gigs in Greenwich Village in 1965. Jimi already displayed extraordinary technical prowess and from the strings of his guitar the blues emerged in a pure form, but at the time America was caught up with beat and with the phenomenal young white musicians associated with it. Ironically, Hendrix found an appreciative and attentive public initially only in the England of the Beatles, where he went thanks to the former member of Animals, Chas Chandler. In 1966 Hendrix conquered Europe with his electrifying, excruciating, and pain-filled singles "Hey Joe" and "Purple Haze," and the sheer power of his concerts. All contributed to the image of Hendrix as a devilish figure caught up with the most extreme experiences of drugs and sex, armed with his Fender Stratocaster guitar, which, from time to time, was transformed into the projection of his

penis or the partner of torrid electric coitus, played with his teeth, elbows and clothes, and rubbed against his microphone stand or against the loudspeakers to obtain the most acid sound possible.

The year 1967 saw the release of *Are You Experienced,* the first extraordinary album of the Jimi Hendrix Experience, the band the guitarist formed with bass player Mitch Mitchell and drummer Noel Redding. Hendrix soon became a superstar with is magical, chaotic music that took the route of psychedelia, enriching it with esoteric references and above all with a wholly new way of playing the guitar. The starting point was the blues, which Hendrix transformed drastically, utilizing every possible technical expedient and solution and every part of his body in order to create the greatest possible number of sounds, voices, and timbre effects with his instrument. In a short time his Fender became the most powerful icon of rock music and his live performances went way beyond anyone's imagination. On June 18, 1967, at the Monterey International Pop Festival, the first of the great rock gatherings, Hendrix concluded his concert by setting his guitar on fire and then smashing it to bits in a sort of ritual that made the audience go wild.

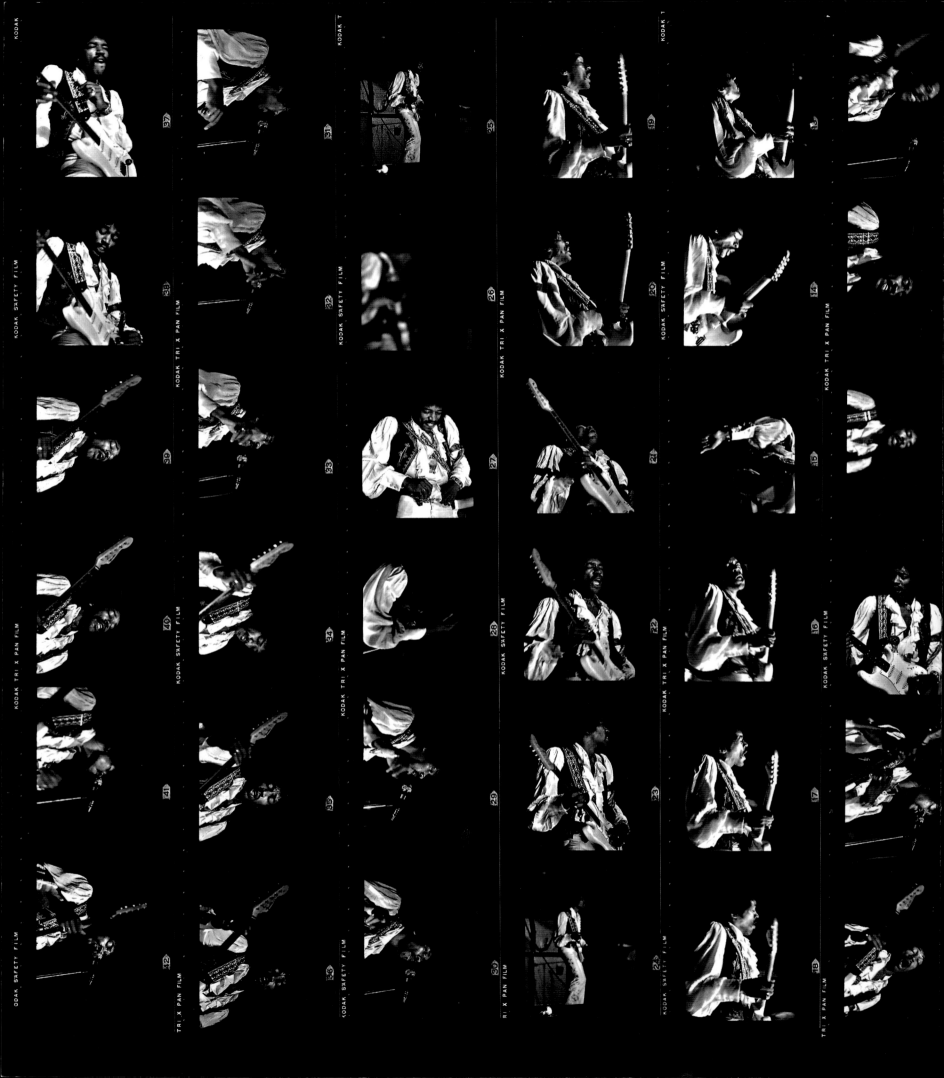

< **The power of the stage** A fine series of photographs of Hendrix performing in a concert held in October 1968. Performing live was what Hendrix enjoyed the most, as the spontaneity of it left ample room for improvisation and direct contact with the audience.

> **Guitar and fire** The concert at the International Pop Festival concert in Monterey, California in 1967 marked Hendrix's debut with the American public after the great success he had enjoyed in London. The performances of the Experience became legendary thanks to the incredible finale of "Wild Thing," when Jimi set his instrument on fire on stage.

JIMI HENDRIX

< **Gibson Flying** Jimi Hendrix's famous Gibson Flying V guitar, which originally was black and then became "psychedelic" after it was painted by Hendrix himself. Jimi had three different Flying Vs, the last one of which was a left-handed guitar customized by Gibson especially for him.

> **A rock icon** Jimi Hendrix has become an icon not only in the history of rock but also of all 20th-century pop culture. His hairstyle, clothing, and performances have been portrayed in thousands of posters, such as this one created by Martin Sharp in 1968.

In August 1968 Hendrix ended the Woodstock Festival by "murdering" the American national anthem, "Star Spangled Banner," producing effects much like bombings and explosions, with the aim of criticizing the Vietnam War unequivocally in music. This concert marked the symbolic end of the decade of great hopes.

Hendrix released only three albums during his short life—*Are You Experienced, Axis: Bold as Love,* and *Electric Ladyland*—but they established his place next to the Beatles and Bob Dylan

as one of the most important figures in the birth and development of rock in the 1960s. Three albums in which the music is nothing like what had come before, where the guitar becomes something more than a musical instrument, the very symbol of rock music.

In 1969 the Jimi Hendrix Experience broke up. Hendrix established the Band of Gypsys with Buddy Miles, thought of collaborating with Miles Davis, took stock of what he had done and looked far

beyond the music he had played until then, and recorded a huge amount of material, trying out musical expressions that were quite different from rock. But he never realized his plans, as he died in 1970 because of an overdose of heroin.

In his amazing journey in search of the definitive sound, Jimi Hendrix used a great many guitars, but they were never a fetish for him, and he gave many of them away to musicians as a gift and either sold or

traded others, remaining "faithful" above all to one model, the Fender Stratocaster. His first guitar dates from 1959 and was a white Supro Orzak that his father gave him and which he played in his first bands. While serving in the army he got hold of a Kay and an Eko, and then persuaded his father to buy him a Danelectro Silverstone. In 1964 he purchased his first Fender, a Duo Sonic, which he used when playing with the Isley Brothers. Later, when he began to work together with Little Richard,

he traded this guitar for a Jazzman, and when he went to play with King Curtis he decided to use a Telecaster. Lastly, in 1966 he opted for a Stratocaster, which, except for a few jam sessions, remained his favorite for quite some time. Hendrix owned a dozen Stratocasters, but the ones that became legendary are those he set on fire in concerts. The first guitar was burned at the Astoria in London in 1967, the second at the Monterey International Pop Festival, once again in 1967, and the third time was in Miami a year later.

< Bakersfield 1968 On October 26, 1968 Jimi Hendrix went on the stage of the Civic Auditorium in Bakersfield, California to perform with a Fender Stratocaster, the guitar that became legendary thanks to him. Over the years, he used about seven different models of Stratocaster.

> Spectacle on the stage Hendrix never failed to make his live concerts as spectacular as possible, and he often played in an unconventional manner, for example holding his guitar behind his back, or he would play with his tongue and teeth, as in this photograph.

Fender Stratocaster

EXPERIENCE

The year 1967 saw the release of
Are You Experienced

Among the other guitars he used were a Gretsch Corvette dating from 1967, a Guild Starfire, a 1955 Les Paul model, a 1968 SG Custom, and three Gibson Flying Vs. In the latter part of his career Hendrix often played with a Flying V, preferring it to his Strato. A master of electric guitar technique, he often used acoustic guitars in the recording studio, among which were a Martin D-45, a Gibson Dove, and a twelve-string Guild.

In the late 1960s Hendrix employed every possible type of special effects with his guitars. The most frequently used ones being a Dallas-Arbiter Fuzz Face, a Mayer Octavia, a Vox wah-wah pedal, a Leslie speaker, and a Univox Univibe, all of which were flanked by dozens of other electric and electronic gadgets. As for amplifiers, he almost always used 100-watt Marshalls, occasionally adopting Sunn and Sun City.

Hendrix is the musician who experimented the most, and most efficiently, with the potential of the electric guitar. He studied the instrument, modified, and analyzed it, handled and touched it and even lived with it as no else had ever done. He transformed the electric guitar into an instrument of unparalleled expressive potential, into a key that opened innumerable doors, into a spaceship able to take listeners outside of space and time. He was not only a "guitarist", he was an inventor, a genius who had no heirs.

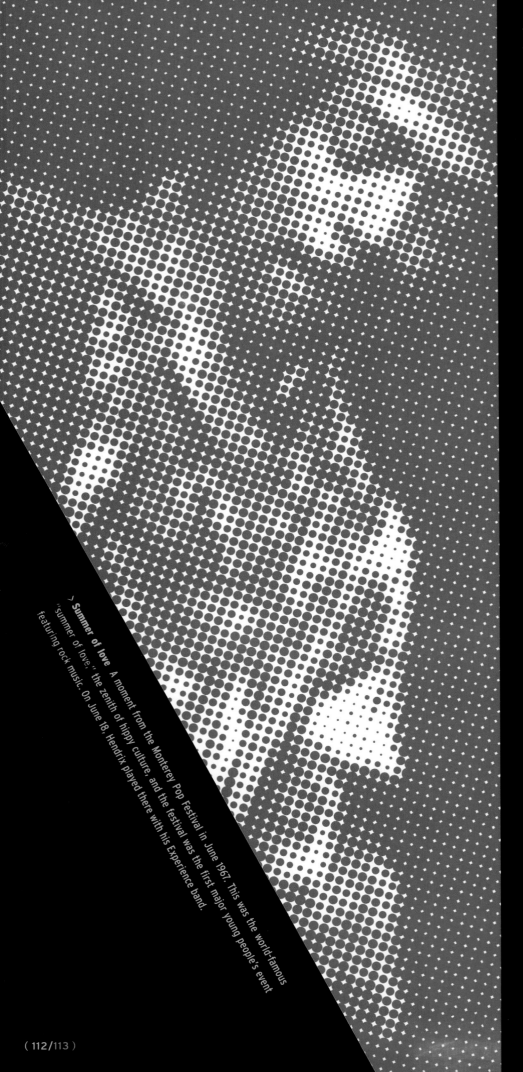

Purple haze,
all in my brain
Lately things just
don't seem the same,
Acting funny,
but I don't know why,
Scuse me while
I kiss the sky.....
(1967 - Purple Haze)

> **Summer of love** A moment from the Monterey Pop Festival in June 1967. This was the world-famous "summer of love," the zenith of hippy culture, and the festival was the first major young people's event featuring rock music. On June 18, Hendrix played there with his Experience band.

JIMMY PAGE

Among the members of Led Zeppelin, Jimmy Page is the one most like the fans of this English band. With a boundless love of their rock music, especially their fourth album, his background was blues music (and in fact, by simplifying, one could say that the type of music played by Led Zeppelin is "hard blues"), but he perfected and broadened his technique, exploring territories that few in the history of rock have penetrated. Possessing almost all the possible techniques (including rather unknown ones such as using a violin bow to play the electric guitar), he utilized tapping and open tuning quite often, thus helping to strengthen the exclusive role of the guitar in rock, particularly in a period in which it was being challenged by the keyboard, which was the protagonist of a new genre that was developing in England. His double-neck Gibson was the very symbol of the central role played by the guitar for him and his band.

Page began his career as a blues guitarist with Yardbirds (the "royal family" of English rock guitarists, boasting the involvement at various times of such famous musicians as Eric Clapton and Jeff Beck) from 1966 to 1968, but we must bear in mind that during his learning stage he not only listened to a lot of African-American music but never forgot British folk music and, like many others of his generation, he was also an exponent of skiffle. Thanks to his extraordinary versatility he was able – both before the birth of Led Zeppelin and during its existence – to play in many sessions of single songs and album recordings by other artists, from Marianne Faithfull's "As Tears Go By" to "Heart of Stone" by the Rolling Stones (in this case, however, it was in an alternate track), the

Them's "Baby Please Don't Go" and the Kinks's first album, and including session work with John Mayall, Nico, Chris Farlowe, Eric Clapton, Joe Cocker, Al Stewart, and even The Who's first single "I Can't Explain" and "Bald Headed Woman" on the reverse side of the same record.

However, Page earned his place in history by playing with Robert Plant, John Paul Jones, and John Bonham in Led Zeppelin, which was born out of the ashes of Yardbirds but went beyond the blues, giving rise to hard rock. Together with Clapton and Hendrix, Page is the main innovator of the rock guitar in the transition period between the late 1960s and early 1970s.

Fender Telecaster
Gibson Les Paul

> **The soul of hard rock** The two "faces" of Led Zeppelin, guitarist Jimmy Page and vocalist Robert Plant, during a performance of the British band in 1973 at the height of its fame.

Following pages

< **Unforgettable solos** Jimmy Page performing with his Gibson Les Paul in 1977. The guitarist became legendary especially for his solo in "Stairway to Heaven," one of the band's most famous and influential songs.

> **A live guitar** Led Zeppelin broke up in 1980, the year this photograph of Jimmy Page was taken. The cause of the breakup was the death of the drummer John Bonham. Rather than find a replacement, Page, Plant, and John Paul Jones decided to disband.

Led Zeppelin
Stairway to Heaven

Yes, there are two paths you can go by
But in the long run
Theres still time to change the road youre on
And it makes me wonder
(1971 - Stairway to Heaven)

He is gifted with remarkable technique, above all with the capacity to create different configurations with his guitar – from the most dream-like to the hard, "metallic" ones – and his powerful style is best exemplified in his unforgettable solos (the one in "Stairway to Heaven" is in first place in the *Guitar World* classification) and his equally crisp, hard-hitting riffs (for example, "Whole Lotta Love" or "Black Dog"). But Page is also able to produce ballads such as "Going To Caifornia" and pieces with oriental overtones such as "Kashmir." Considered almost a divine musician after the discovery of his links with black magic and certain occult practices, Page is extremely popular and widely imitated for his ability to combine moments of tenderness with aggressive episodes that make him – and Led Zeppelin in general – the only tangible sign of rock that is still alive and topical, surpassing even the Rolling Stones.

< Guitar and violin bow Page has always played his instrument in innovative ways to obtain original sounds, using both electric and electronic effects and also, as can be seen in this photo, a violin bow.

> Reunions Jimmy Page in a 1977 concert. After Bonham's death, Led Zeppelin played together only twice: in 1985 for the Live Aid concert, and in 2008 for a one-shot concert with Jason Bonham, the famous drummer's son, playing the drums.

KEITH RICHARDS

Considered by many to be the "riff king" because of the great number of popular riffs he produced in over 45 years with the Rolling Stones, which is why he has earned the nickname of "Riff Richards," Keith Richards has often described himself, and rightly so, as a purely rhythmic guitarist who is very much attached to the acoustic dimension of the instrument, even though with time he came to use electric guitars to quite an extent. He owns more than 1000, most of which were given to him, but he always uses the same ones, mainly Fender (Telecaster and Stratocaster) and Gibson (ES-355), always maintaining the same sound. He has often joked about this, saying that he is able to make any guitar sound the same.

Greatly inspired by the marvelous American rhythm and blues of Bo Diddley and Chuck Berry, in the early 1960s, together with Mick Jagger, he transferred that type of musical feeling into the English beat milieu, creating a new and different way of conceiving two-guitar accompaniment, which, beginning with the success of "Satisfaction," would in turn conquer the American public. This is a type of rhythm in which the parts shared by the two guitarists are not set but are rather interchangeable and often superimposed. Backed up first by Brian Jones, then Mick Taylor and finally Ron Wood, his manner of playing and tuning the guitar (usually open G tuning) led to a "musical rebirth" at the end of the 1960s, as he himself stated. Open tuning in fact reduces the number of notes and allowed him to concentrate on rhythm and riffs. He himself made a comment to the effect that in order to play

blues you need only three strings and a damned fool to play on them.

His entire career revolves around the musical and personal story of the Rolling Stones, with whom he has played since he was quite young; not only has he never abandoned the group but is its driving force. He also developed a brief career as a soloist with the Xpensive Winos, more than anything else as a response to Jagger's ventures as a solo artist and the latter's lack of interest in the destiny of the Stones. As a soloist, Richards has released only one album of unpublished material, the very solid and entertaining *Talk Is Cheap*, and one live recording, *Live at the Hollywood Palladium*. Both releases help us to understand even more how the Rolling Stones cannot exist without his guitar and how rock music learned from him, more than from his duets with Jagger, the basic rules of its existence. When he dominates the scene without Mick, Keith does not seem at all intimidated; quite the contrary, he even plays at being a singer with surprising understatement.

Keith Richards

Perfectly integrated into a period marked by experimention with drugs and hallucinatory substances and later becoming the very symbol and pop icon of a lifestyle marked by excesses and self-destruction, Richards – with his hollow cheeks and wrinkles and his pride in wearing shabby clothes – has never stopped proclaiming his addiction to all kinds of drugs and all types of guitars, even though his excessive use of illegal substances has often jeopardized his creativity as well as his personal life. Despite everything, he is and will always be the rock guitarist *par excellence*. It does not matter if his technique is not refined; the fact that his solos are not legendary is of little importance; and it is irrelevant that the distance between him and the legendary rock guitarists is huge. Keith Richards *is* rock guitar in the deepest, most basic and essential sense of this genre. Without Richards and his riffs and rhythmical guitar playing, rock would not have been the same.

< Sympathy for the Devil One of the most important moments in the history of the Stones is celebrated in this photograph of Keith Richards and Mick Jagger at the Olympic Studios in London during the recording of "Sympathy for the Devil," which was filmed by one of the masters of Nouvelle Vague cinema, Jean-Luc Godard, in 1968.

> Tour of the Americas, 1975 The perfect couple of English rock guitarists, Keith Richards and Ronnie Wood, while tuning their instruments backstage during the Rolling Stones' 1975 tour, a short time after "Woody" had joined the band.

Well, then what can a poor boy do
Except to sing for a rock'n'roll band
'Cause in sleepy London town
There's no place for a street fighting man
No!
Get down
(1968 - Street Fighting Man)

Preceding pages

< **A 1979 concert** Keith Richards during a performance, enveloped in a cloud of smoke. The guitarist's lifestyle triggered many a problem with drugs and alcohol, but it also inspired the character of Jack Sparrow interpreted by Johnny Depp in the movie *Pirates of the Caribbean*.

> **The rock guitarist** Keith Richards performing with the Stones in 1971 with a transparent guitar, an Ampeg Dan Armstrong in plexiglas. In this period he played next to Mick Taylor.

< > **Riff Richards** Keith Richards's nickname is Riff Richards, because he invented for the Rolling Stones innumerable guitar riffs, his specialty as a rock composer, which became standards for entire generations.

Gibson Les Paul
Fender Telecaster
Gibson Firebird

PETE TOWNSHEND

The Who

A musician who has made history by being the first and greatest destroyer of musical instruments on stage and also for the great influence he has had on the development of rock music, Pete Townshend has been and continues to be the very soul of The Who. With his "overpowered" guitar based on rhythm and accompaniment and, at the beginning of his career, only slightly mindful of the solo parts, he has offered a unique sound to the famous band by merging his guitar sound perfectly with the rhythmical section (bass and drums). Often undervalued (while Clapton, Hendrix, and Richards are always mentioned in the lists of the great guitarists of the 1960s, he is frequently neglected), Townshend is a creator of amazing riffs, an excellent and rock-solid composer, and a guitarist who over

the years has developed a highly personal style, above all in its rhythmical aspects but also in the solos, which are never fruitlessly spectacular and have become more and more refined on a technical level. He is also a guitar showman who has developed a "windmill" style with his right arm worthy of the best bowling players, a sensational gesture that has characterized his persona on stage as much as the ritual destruction of the instrument itself.

Greatly interested in spiritual matters, and in particular a follower of the Indian master Meher Baba since 1968, Pete Townshend has become deeply involved in oriental religions, which has not prevented him from experimenting with drugs, both light and heavy. It has not stopped him from smashing all kinds of guitars, from the Rickenbeckers of his early career to the cheaper Fenders (both Stratocasters and Telecasters), up to the Gibson SGs (like the one he smashed to pieces at Woodstock) and Les Pauls.

It was exactly the ritual demolition of the musical instruments during the live performances of The Who that caused more than one problem for Townshend. He has said that after singing and playing "My Generation" it would make no sense if the band did not destroy everything, but the first time he smashed his guitar against the amplifier during a concert in Germany, Townshend found himself confronted with a gun that was pointed at him by a policeman who ordered him to stop immediately. Furthermore, in 1967, while performing during the broadcast of the Smothers Brothers Comedy Hour, when all the band members destroyed their instruments, Townshend was too close to the powerful electric charge that Keith Moon had placed in his drum set when it exploded. Now this accident is often cited as one of the causes of the guitarist's partial deafness, another cause being his constant exposure to loud music, especially during The Who's concert at the Charlton Athletic Football Club in 1976, which was cited in the *Guinness Book of Records* for over a decade as the performance with the highest volume level ever recorded during a concert.

Townshend's story is the story of his band, The Who,

which has British roots but is "American" as regards its success and eccentric showmanship. He has been capable of evoking the dreams and delusions of an entire generation, of producing two legendary rock operas, *Tommy* and *Quadrophenia,* of creating riffs that have become historic, and of realizing one of the albums that any guitarist should learn by heart, *Who's Next.* But he has also made many albums as a soloist, including the first-rate *Empty Glass,* released in 1980.

In any case, a few chords on his guitar are enough to show us what rock is and has been.

> **A legendary guitarist** A fine portrait of the artist as a young man, in 1966, at the height of the "mod" explosion led by The Who. Small Faces and Townshend's band were the favorites among this group of British youngsters.

This guitar has seconds to live.

< The kids are allright The poster advertising the film *The Kids Are Alright,* with Pete Townshend about to destroy his guitar and the phrase "This guitar has seconds to live." The movie came out in 1979.

> USA, 1967 Pete Townshend throwing his guitar in the air during a concert of The Who held in August 1967 in Flint, Michigan. The Who became extremely popular in the United States and to this day have a huge following.

People try to put us d-down
Just because we get around
Things they do look awful c-cold
I hope I die before I get old

This is my generation
This is my generation, baby
(1965 - My Generation)

< London, 1967 The Who performing in the Savile Theatre, London in 1967. Pete Townshend is playing a double-neck Gibson EDS-1275. He did not use this instrument for very long, even though the Gibson was his favorite guitar for most of the 1970s.

< **Spectacular leaps** Pete Townshend and the drummer Keith Moon on stage with The Who in 1975. The photograph does justice to Townshend's stage antics, as he prances and swings his arm and makes spectacular leaps, which became trademark features of his performances.

> **London, 1981** Another of Pete Townshend's leaps, this time at the Wembley Arena in 1981. Behind the drums is Kenny Jones, who was later replaced by Zack Starkey, Ringo Starr's son.

RITCHIE BLACKMORE

For an entire generation the name Richie Blackmore was synonymous with "rock guitar." Not because Blackmore had become a rival of the guitar heroes such as Hendrix, Clapton, Townshend, and Richards, just to mention a few, but rather because with Deep Purple he laid down the ground rules of hard rock and established how the sound and style of electric guitar solos would evolve in the future. As absurd as it may seem, while Jimi Hendrix has few imitators, the world is full of followers of Richie Blackmore, musicians who have thoroughly understood his lesson and have gone on to develop their own personal style. However, it must be said in fact that most of them have not followed his example correctly, and have become super-technical show-offs, able to play a huge amount of notes in a ridiculously short time, while others have understood that Blackmore's style consisted more of expression than speed and that excessive theatrical antics came to the fore in the history of guitar playing only when creativity had begun to wane. It would therefore be difficult not to include Blackmore among the masters of the electric guitar in the 1960s and 1970s, and impossible not to learn some of his most memorable riffs by heart (for instance, for an electric guitarist learning the notes of "Smoke on the Water" is like learning so say "mommy" when one is a child). His influential position is due to the success he earned with Deep Purple and Rainbow, as well as the "non-rock" Blackmore's Night project, but even more so it is due to his being a complete, original, spectacular and, above all in the early part of his career, innovative guitarist.

One need only listen to a concert by Blackmore's Night to discover his musical ability through his present love for refined and classicizing pop, in which we will find melodies, rhythms, and sounds of centuries-old music, and in which Blackmore almost never plays the electric guitar and concentrates on precision. This is music light years away from the hard rock that made him justly famous as one of the great heroes of the electric guitar in the 1970s.

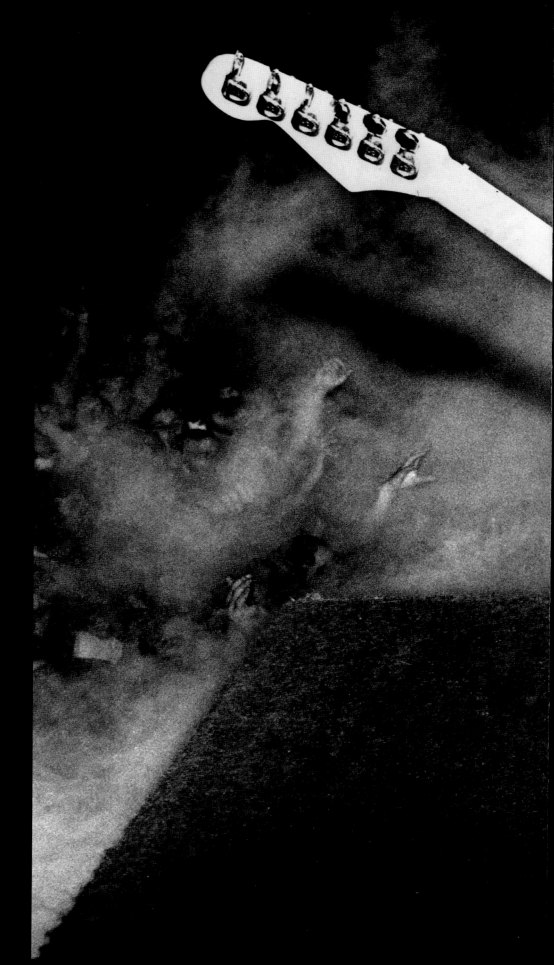

< > California Jam Tour, 1974 An "athletic" gesture on the part of
Richie Blackmore, who smashes his guitar against the amplifier during
the 1974 California Jam Tour with Deep Purple, who became legends in
the States.

Fender Stratocaster

We all came out to Montreux on the Lake Geneva shoreline
To make records with a mobile - We didn't have much time
Frank Zappa & the Mothers were at the best place around
But some stupid with a flare gun burned the place to the ground
Smoke on the water - A fire in the sky.
(1972 - Smoke on the Water)

< **Deep Purple in Rock** Richie Blackmore during the 1973 tour of Deep Purple. The band's masterpiece is still *Deep Purple in Rock*, dating to 1970, but it was with the guitar riff in "Smoke on the Water" (1972) that Richie Blackmore reached the height of his fame.

> **Tension** Blackmore is immortalized here performing during his 1974 tour in the United States. The following year the guitarist left the band for the first time because of rifts with the other members.

ANGUS YOUNG

AC/DC's guitarist Angus McKinnon Young will go down in history not only for his talent but also for his totally original style, which is seemingly foreign to the world of hard rock even though he is one of its leading exponents. His schoolboy outfit and cap (presumably the one from Ashfield Boys High School, which he attended), his inseparable "devil schoolboy" guitar (a Gibson 1968 SG), and his "paso doble," a choreographic move that – as is the case with Michael Jackson's moonwalk – remains his signature trademark recognized throughout the world. Young stated that his band likes to offer a show, and if the people in the audience have spent a lot of money then they deserve to hear and see something really special. AC/DC is "his" band and it has never distinguished itself for sophisticated music, but rather expressed the essence of hard rock with the basic, incessant rhythm in which Angus Young himself introduces more complex blues-style passages.

"Professor Riff," as he has been called because of his explosive creations, such as "Highway to Hell," is only five feet tall and his fingers are certainly long and tapering as one would expect from a guitarist. He is one of the fastest and most dazzling guitarists of all, especially in consideration of the fact that he has never used special effects to any degree and has always been faithful to his Gibson, trying to draw the maximum from this instrument without resorting to any other expedient than his hands. However, it is the simplicity and immediacy of his riffs that are his trademark: "I must admit that inventing a riff is usually easier than searching for a melody or a nice passage." And he prefers the primitive sound of the early rockers to that of the more sophisticated performers who followed. He once said that Clapton had been described to him as a unique and incomparable master. "Nonsense! Chuck Berry on a good day beats him out of sight whenever he wants to."

Angus was born in Glasgow, Scotland in 1955, the younger brother of George Young, a member of the Easybeats. He moved to Australia with his family and in 1973 founded AC/DC together with his brother Malcolm and singer Bon Scott. And since then they have waged a battle against disco and punk music with such historic albums as *Let There Be Rock* (1977), *Highway to Hell* (1979), *Back in Black* (1980) and *For Those about to Rock We Salute You* (1981).

< **An historic group** Phil Rudd, Mark Evans, Angus Young, Malcolm Young, and Bon Scott: the legendary formation of AC/DC, which attained its first success in the first half of the 1970s. This photograph was taken at the WEA offices in 1976.

> **Milk and rock 'n' roll** Angus Young trying to disprove the myth of "sex, drugs and rock 'n' roll" by drinking a glass of milk during his band's first international press conference, which was held in 1976, the year he signed his first recording contract with Atlantic.

< **In uniform** Guitarist Angus Young playing at the Reading Festival, one of the principal English music events, in 1976. Here he is performing with his favorite instrument of that period, a Gibson Sg.

> **London, 1979** The inventor of extraordinary and very simple riffs, Angus Young is an extremely solid and creative guitarist, qualities that emerge above all in his live performances. Here he is on stage at the Hammersmith Odeon, London in 1979.

Gibson SG

‹ › **The heart of AC/DC** Young is the driving spirit of AC\DC, whose sound revolves around that produced by his electric guitar. He is also the band's most spectacular performer, always wearing the short pants and cap that are his trademark costume.

BRIAN MAY

Of all the great guitarists, Brian May is certainly the one whose beginnings and background would not have suggested a future in music. He had planned to become an astrophysicist and in the late 1960s his studies at Imperial College London seemed to point toward a career as an analyst of interplanetary dust. However, the music world was lying in wait just around the corner in the form of his meeting with the eclectic Freddie Mercury and with the already fairly well-known drummer Roger Taylor, who were members of the Smile and May bands (and who worked together with bass player John Deacon at a later stage), which led to the formation of the band that became known as Queen.

From 1971, when "Queen I" was formed, to 1974, when the band recorded the album *A Night At The Opera*, the Brian May–Freddie Mercury duo experimented with and broadened the horizons of rock music by utilizing various styles and techniques, eventually merging them all in Queen's seminal creation, "Bohemian Rhapsody."

From that time on the driving force of the band seemed to fade away gradually, as did its creativity, which began to become repetitive. Although the musicians continued their experimentation, its intensity and importance progressively decreased. However, this did not prevent Brian May from being considered a pivotal guitarist who is able to compose solos with simple melodies and technical fascination that are truly unique (a classic example of which is the one in "We Will Rock You," based only on rhythm) as well as one of the founders of the delay effect (that is, the effect whereby the guitar repeats a certain sound as an echo), a masterful instance of which can be heard in "Brighton Rock." His style is over-elaborate and "baroque," but this is exactly why it is so spectacular and has had such an extraordinary impact on an entire generation of guitarists who operate somewhere between hard rock and pop.

Brian May's sound is one of the easiest to recognize, partly because he made his Red Special guitar himself from a late 18th-century mantelpiece and used the spare parts of a bicycle and a motorbike for the electric components. Another interesting aspect of the Brian May sound is that he usually plays with a smoothed six pence piece instead of a plectrum in order to produce a rougher, more electric tone.

Often the highly spectacular nature of his solos has made up for large gaps in creativity, but there is no doubt that his style has been of fundamental importance for hosts of rock guitarists from the 1970s on. However, in 2007, after years and years of success as a rock star, May finally completed his Ph.D. thesis and at the end of the same year he was appointed chancellor of Imperial College.

Red Special (custom-built)

< **Unforgettable solos** Brian May playing his guitar in front of drummer Roger Taylor at a Queen concert in 1978. Brian May's solos had a great influence on dozens of hard rock guitarists of the 1970s.

> **Rome, 2005** Brian May performing with Queen on April 4, 2005 at the Palalottomatica Hall, Rome. The concert held by the English band was one of the few that were not cancelled after the death of Pope John Paul II.

Following pages

< **Clean, precise sound** Brian May performs in 1980. The English guitarist has a style based on the speed and clarity of his lengthened and slightly distorted sound, which over the years has become richer and more complex.

> **May and Mercury** The golden couple of Queen were the vocalist Freddy Mercury, who died in 1991, and guitarist Brian May, here performing in 1982. The understanding between May and Mercury led to the success of Queen, which always achieved a perfect blend of rock and melody.

TONY IOMMI

Generally speaking, speculation as to the origins of a particular musical form almost always leads to contradictions and very rarely is agreement reached on a single, acceptable hypothesis. This issue hardly ever arises when it comes to discussing the birth of heavy metal. It is a genre that was born, fully complete in all its aspects, with the music of Black Sabbath and, in particular, in the sinister riffs produced by Tony Iommi.

The left-handed guitarist, though often overshadowed in terms of notoriety and stage presence by frontman Ozzy Osbourne, was chiefly responsible for the heaviness and gloom that was to render the sound of the Birmingham group so unique. His in fact are the darkest and most terrifying riffs composed in the 1970s, and as a result constantly imitated by countless, long-haired followers dressed in leather and studs. "Paranoid," "Iron Man," "Electric Funeral," and "Children of The Grave" constitute his heaviest legacy, even though his discography also frequently includes passages that are sweet, even melancholic, if not exactly psychedelic ("Planet Caravan," "Solitude").

A characteristic of his style that cannot be overlooked is the frequent use of the tritone, a powerfully evocative musical "formula" the origins of which have always been surrounded by legendary rumors of supposed connections with dark forces. It was precisely this adoption of the *Diabolus In Musica* (the medieval definition of tritone), coupled with the use of horror-related themes, that transformed a piece such as "Black Sabbath" into a true heavy metal manifesto.

Tony Iommi is a classic example of how to turn weaknesses into strengths. He has never been an exceptional guitar player, on top of which he is missing several finger bones in his right hand (a legacy of his past as a factory worker), but he nevertheless managed to create one of the most distinctive and most imitated of all the playing styles in the history of rock. His name is forever linked with Black Sabbath, where he remained as the one and only fixture for over 30 years, starting with its debut as a blues group (with the name Earth) and then subsequently sharing all its high and low points as the band went through all its innumerable permutations. His solo debut appeared only in 2000 with the album *Iommi*, a record which was essentially a parade of stars, bringing together three generations of hard rock music. It was a late but certainly well-deserved tribute to a man who had undoubtedly been the "heaviest" guitarist of all times.

Gibson SG

< **Down-tuning** Tony Iommi performing with Ozzy Osbourne and Black Sabbath in 1978. The English guitarist is playing a JayDee Sg. He always tunes down his guitar, first in D sharp, then in C sharp, to produce a deeper sound.

> **Paranoid, 1970** Black Sabbath at a concert held in 1970, the year they released their first album, which remains their most important and most successful one, *Paranoid*, for Vertigo. The guitar riffs played by Iommi were a major feature of the album.

MICK RONSON

> **London, 1973** This was the year when the character of Ziggy Stardust created by David Bowie took his last bow on stage. Up to that time, he had been flanked by the guitarist in the Spiders from Mars, Mick Ronson.

The musician and producer Mick Ronson was much more than David Bowie's guitarist. His guest appearances with various stars of British rock in the early 1970s (including the dazzling guitar playing in the first version of Elton John's "Madman Across the Water") were flanked by his activity as Bowie's arranger, beginning with the album *The Man Who Sold the World,* which was followed by the seminal *The Rise and Fall of Ziggy Stardust.* Enamored of Italian melody (he recorded "Music is Lethal," the British version of Battisti's "Vorrei, non vorrei, ma se vuoi," with lyrics by Bowie himself), Ronson could produce truly lyrical solos that were never exaggerated and never exceeded the limits of the glam rock of that period. He was a truly complete and "musical" musician, and besides the sound of his Les Paul guitar he imparted personality to the works of several artists. For instance, the violin parts in Lou Reed's "Satellite of Love" and "Perfect Day" are his.

What is more, Ronson often played the piano, thus contributing to a total sound that benefited both Bowie's and Reed's production and that made some of their works amazingly similar, at least from the standpoint of instrumentation.

Like other highly qualified guitarists with a solid musical education, Ronson – who first wanted to become a cellist after having played several different instruments in his youth – was living proof that even in rock music constant practicing always results in something that is original and of a high level of quality, head and shoulders above what is usually in circulation. However, this does not necessarily mean being limited to technique alone, as Ronson demonstrated throughout his career. Again, with Bowie he was the very essence of

the rock guitarist, the ideal colleague for any star – as well as being a star in his own right – able to accompany and support the vocalist and at the same time upstage him when called for. He was an irreplaceable sideman capable of being a frontman absolutely indispensable for a perfect rendition of "Ziggy Stardust & The Spiders from Mars."

Ronson was one of the great rock guitarists. His version of "Like a Rolling Stone" on a posthumous album, *Heaven and Hull,* is perhaps the most beautiful and most "rock" of all.

< Glam rock The farewell performance of Ziggy Stardust and the Spiders from Mars at the Hammersmith Odeon, London on July 3, 1973. Ronson, with his look and guitar style, established the canons of glam rock. At Ronson's side is David Bowie.

> Guitarist and producer Mick Ronson collaborated with many other musicians besides David Bowie, including Lou Reed (whose album *Transformer* he produced), Morrissey, and Elton John. He was one of the most influential of British guitarists.

Gibson Les Paul

RY COODER

More than just a musician, Ry Cooder could perhaps best be described as a musicologist. Notwithstanding the fair number of records he has produced and the no less insignificant number of collaborative ventures undertaken during the 1960s (from the Rolling Stones' "Love In Vain" and "Sister Morphine," to Van Morrison's "Full Force Gale"), the most defining feature of his career was to be his exploration of the roots of American music, mainly through three fundamental aspects: locations, instruments, and content.

Blessed with great technique and a distinct inclination towards virtuosity, Cooder has always covered all the genres, chasing regional and ancient music and playing styles, ranging from the Hawaiian to the more strictly Texan, from blues to Dixieland, from country to R&B. His guitar, often using a slide, was played to accommodate all styles; he was always looking for the modern touch and the pieces that were likely to benefit from repetition. The

phase given over to experimentation only truly began after his solo debut in 1970, with an album carrying his own name as the title. This phase reached its peak with the two records *Paradise and Lunch and Chicken Skin Music*, where gospel and soul blend together with typically white overtones.

The turning point in Cooder's career arrived in the 1980s, when he became a composer of soundtracks for major film productions, dividing his time between full-blown Hollywood-style movies (*Streets of Fire and Mississipi Adventure* by Walter Hill) and art-house films (notably *Paris, Texas* by Wim Wenders). Even in this field, he brought with him his reverence for the roots of North American music, along with a passion for re-evaluating long abandoned

styles and for extending the limits of existing genres by mixing them with new influences.

Finally, in the 1990s, Cooder was largely responsible for the rediscovery of Compay Segundo and particularly the Buena Vista Social Club, a group of Cuban musicians that were only known (and not widely so) in their own country, and who, thanks to the attention drawn to them by the American guitarist along with his director friend Wim Wenders in the documentary film *Buena Vista Social Club*, became a worldwide success.

FRANK ZAPPA

The world of guitar lovers is split in two. On the one hand there are those who think Frank Zappa was one of the greatest guitarists of all time, while the others feel he was self-centered and not at all interesting. Those who uphold the latter view are certain that Zappa was much more innovative and gifted as a composer than as a guitarist, and that, like all musicians who play several instruments, he never developed an exceptional technique or sensibility for any one of them — even though he was naturally talented as a percussionist, as is demonstrated by the fact that he always preferred to have musicians better than himself playing with

him (for instance, the guitarist Steve Vai). As proof of their theory that Zappa was a better composer than guitar player, his detractors point to the works dominated by the Synclavier (a hybrid instrument combining a synthesizer and a sampler that was utilized quite a lot by the more experimental musicians from the late 1970s on), or to those featuring an entire orchestra that plays passages that were not, however, composed on the guitar (the most extraordinary example being *The Yellow Shark,* 1993).

In point of fact, Zappa was one of the greatest electric guitarists in the history of popular music, an extraordinary soloist who preferred expression to technique and who combined his talent as a composer with his instrumental skills in an oeuvre that was both complex and complete. The guitar was the instrument he loved most. He dedicated the double album *Guitar* to this instrument, as well

as many other albums recorded live (the series *Shut Up 'N Play Yer Guitar*), and composed many masterpieces for it, first and foremost the legendary "Watermelon in Easter Hay" (in which he combines his gifts for melody and asymmetrical tempi), as well as a large number of appealing riff-refrains such as "I'm the Slime," "Camarillo Brillo," and "Muffin Man."

Zappa's favorite instrument was the electric guitar, which he played aggressively and with determination. It is curious to note that in his work he strives for completeness but he seems to pay no attention to the acoustical and intimate qualities of this instrument.

Zappa probably knew he was a fine guitarist, despite all the manias of the technicians of this instrument, who often accused him of being too "verbose," of unwarranted self-glorification, and of being unbearably obsessed with

solos. At a certain stage of almost all Zappa's concert peformances there was the inevitable solo, usually improvised, that might last much more than one would legitimately expect. But his greatness as an electric guitarist lies precisely in this "unpredictability," in his only real obsession, that of achieving the "perfect" solo, in which technique, expressivity, and improvisation are merged into one, able to surpass any other musical form. It is certainly no accident that Zappa served as an example and inspired so many guitarists who gained experience with him and developed some of his ideas, first and foremost Steve Vai and Adrian Belew.

Information is not knowledge
Knowledge is not wisdom
Wisdom is not truth
Truth is not beauty
Beauty is not love
Love is not music / MUSIC IS THE BEST

(1979 - Joe's Garage)

< **Debut** In 1966, the year this photo was taken in Copenhagen, Frank Zappa made his debut on the rock stage with his first album, *Freak Out*. With the guitarist is the extraordinary Mothers of Invention band.

> **Overdubbing** Frank Zappa during a 1976 concert held in New York City. In many of Zappa's records there are guitar solos that he had played in live performances and then "overdubbed" onto the studio recordings.

< **Obsession with solos** Frank Zappa will surely remain one of the leading figures in 20th-century music, both because of his amazing gift for composing and his great talent as a guitarist, which is manifested above all in the album *Shut up and Play Your Guitar*.

> **Ironic and transgressive** Frank Zappa performs in New York at Halloween in 1981. Sarcastic and quite removed from all vogues and trends, Zappa even poked fun at the very nature of rock and pop music in many of his ironic and transgressive lyrics.

GARY MOORE

< **Preferably with a Gibson** Gary Moore photographed in the 1970s, at the dawn of a period in which English rock, which was greatly influenced by American blues, began to develop thanks to a new generation of electric guitarists.

< **Somewhere between blues and rock** Gary Moore in London in 1984. He has played with many bands, from Skid Row to Thin Lizzy and Colosseum, and has also made many solo albums that have been a great success throughout Europe.

> **A metal approach** Blues were always the musical heart of the style of Gary Moore, who continued to improve his technique and expressive qualities throughout his career, becoming one of the most highly appreciated guitarists in the world.

Part of Gary Moore's career was spent with the Skid Row band, another part with the more noteworthy Thin Lizzy; he was leader of the Gary Moore Band, then played in a duo with Greg Lake and later with B. B. King, Albert King, and Albert Collins. Gary Moore has left no stones unturned in his musical career, having tried several genres (even a dance music phase that is better forgotten), but his first and only love has always been the blues, which he prefers to play with Gibson guitars. In fact, he was one of the first recognized by this historic guitar-maker with a signature model, which by the way was not a reproduction of an existing model, but a totally new guitar made to suit his needs.

Yet it was another guitar model that had the most impact on the musical life of Gary Moore. He had entered the music scene as the protégé of Peter Green of Fleetwood Mac, who looked after the youngster much like a godfather. In fact, Moore was able to buy Green's mythical Les Paul guitar with a nasal sound for a ridiculous price (the same price Gary had paid for his guitar) when the latter decided to abandon his musical career. Gifted with great technique as well as considerable expressivity, Moore has always been torn between the blues tradition and the "metallic" approach to rock music. As a soloist he has concentrated more on the former passion, while when he played with Skid Row he enjoyed greater success, but also abandoned many of his characteristic features (his light and rapid touch) in favor of a more spectacular performance.

Recently, Moore's contribution to the history of blues rock was acknowledged when Marshall asked him to make a testimonial for the return on the market of the Bluesbreaker Combo, the amplifiers that Eric Clapton had originally made famous.

JOE PERRY

American rock has produced many great guitarists and spectacular soloists, songwriters, and innovators who are both highly technical and extremely creative. But there can be no doubt that among the elite of American guitarists a place must be reserved for Joe Perry. A soloist of average stature, Perry epitomizes the more classic and traditional rock guitarist, somewhat like Keith Richards. He is able to excite his audience with a few chords, some riffs, his outstanding stage presence, and robust rhythmical tension. Perry was and is the soul of Aerosmith, which has been the foremost interpreter of the transition from epic to commercial rock without losing sight of quality and authenticity, the success and evolution of which is based precisely on the sound of his guitar.

Perry's co-leader of Aerosmith – the other half of the so-called Toxic Twins – is Steven Tyler, and the two musicians have been together, through thick and thin, for almost 40 years. In fact, from 1969 to 1979 Aerosmith enjoyed moderate success with melodic rock that stemmed from the music of the Rolling Stones and the American tradition. Fundamental factors of the group's sound were Joe Perry and his guitar with its sober, melancholic tone.

With his constant companion, a Gibson Les Paul, Joe Perry has been both on stage and in the recording studio the heart of the band's creativity, so much so that when in 1979 a heated argument backstage among the musicians' wives forced Joe to leave Aerosmith, the group had to disband. Perry went on to form the Joe Perry Project, cutting three albums that enjoyed some degree of success (the last one with the pithy title *Once a Rocker, Always a Rocker*).

However, the greatest moment in the career of Aerosmith was yet to come. Dissatisfied with being obliged to play on his own for such a long time, in 1984 Perry returned to his old band and they produced a remake of their 1975 hit "Walk This Way." This highly modern version incorporated rap and was a collaboration with Run-DMC. This mixture of traditional rock and the new language of rap marked not only the comeback of the band on the musical scene, but also one of the most important symbolic moments in rock music of the 1980s. From that time on Tyler and Perry began a second childhood, so to speak, and a long period of success that allowed the guitarist to regain his rank as one of the stars of American rock guitarists. Perry also cut a solo disk in 2005 in his Boston studio. For the first time the band had only one member, Perry, who played all the instruments, which was very rewarding for him on a personal level and was also applauded by the critics and public alike, earning him a Grammy nomination.

< > **The beginnings of Aerosmith** Joe Perry and Tom Hamilton in 1970. The two musicians founded Aerosmith in Boston, together with Steven Tyler, Joey Kramer, and Ray Tabano. Two years later, when Ray Whitford replaced Tabano, they recorded their first album.

Gibson Les Paul

< The Joe Perry Project In the late 1970s, Joe Perry left Aerosmith because of a dispute with Tom Hamilton and went on to found his own band, the Joe Perry Project. He returned to Aerosmith in the mid-1980s. This photograph was taken in 1988.

> Joe and Steven The duo that is the heart and soul of Aerosmith consists of the guitarist Joe Perry and the vocalist Steven Tyler A collaboration that in many ways is similar to the one between Keith Richards and Mick Jagger in the Rolling Stones.

Walk this way, walk this way just gimme a kiss like this! (1975 - Walk This Way)

< > **Madison Square Garden, New York, 1997** An Aerosmith concert held in 1997. In its "second life" Aerosmith became an electric pop band with a tremendous impact that produced hit after hit throughout the 1990s.

NEIL YOUNG

We have had Elvis, the Beatles, Bob Dylan, the Rolling Stones, punk, electronic, country, psychedelic music, grunge, and new wave, and in the meantime rock has changed, died, and been reborn several times. But from 1966 to the present the only person who has faithfully followed the ups and downs of the history of rock, who has celebrated and lived through the changes of young people's culture, who has desperately and intelligently tried to make sense of the world and sound of rock is Neil Young. The bard of desperation and joy, the adventurous and solitary Neil Young has plunged into the depths of a musical language as few others have done. He has succeeded in becoming a songwriter, singer, and musician all in one, both an experimenter and a traditionalist. He has combined the best and worst of a young culture marked by sensational defeats and thrilling conquests.

Young's nickname "Shakey" was invented by his friends, who made fun of the "steady hand" he had when making home movies of children, wives, and the usual things one shoots in these personal videos. But that hand is also the one that, more than any other hand in the world, has created sounds with an electric guitar that stir and lacerate one's soul. The music of this Canadian rocker consists basically of passion, power and feelings, and demands an equally passionate effort on the part of his listeners. Those who are looking for smooth, glossy music, elegant sound, and songs suitable for present-day radio programs will certainly not be satisfied with Young's songs, or his guitar style. But those who still want to find meaning in rock and in music in general, those who are looking for a good reason why they should buy a record, should listen to this "old" Canadian gentleman who is so hopelessly out of date and let themselves be carried away by the sound of his guitar and accept the passionately imperfect notes of his solos as "definitive." His solos are long, indeed interminable, deeply expressive, and light years away from all forms of ostentation, technical prowess, and rapid execution. Young's solos go straight to the heart; they are vibrant and electrifying and drive the guitar well beyond obvious technical and tonal solutions. All this is obtained with a device that Young has dubbed "the Whizzer," an effects box placed in front of his feet that has a great many "gadgets" that can be combined without lessening the sound quality of the guitar. And this is not all: Young controls the volume of the amplifier of the guitar itself and uses an amplification "package" that consists of a Magnatone, a large transistor Baldwin Exterminator, a Fender Reverb Unit, as well as the crucial component, a 1959 Fender Delux amplifier, his favorite ("I couldn't play without it."). In fact, he owns 156 examples of this model, all identical, but according to Young none of them plays as well as the original. While he prefers simple, low-cost acoustic guitars, which, as he himself admits, he uses to write most of his pieces, the electric guitar he loves and uses most is his "Old Black," a Les Paul Gold Top dated 1953 that some former owner painted black.

This combination makes Young the noisiest, wildest, most unpredictable guitarist in the history of rock, a musician who, like Dr. Jekyll and Mr. Hyde, has two parallel lives. The first is that of the acoustic musician, the "balladeer," the songwriter and singer, who is melodic, romantic, and "conservative," while the second is the rocker, the fearless and blameless "lone rider" who can play the electric guitar like no one else, the only true heir of the Hendrix school. Young's adventure with the Buffalo Springfield band and Crosby, Stills and Nash, and above all his career as a soloist have taken him through many different phases. But sooner or later he has always returned to his electric guitar, to his interminable solos, and to those searing explosions of energy that only he can offer to the public.

It should come as no surprise, therefore, that the younger generations and the latest wave of rockers consider Young unique, the only "dinosaur" of the 1960s that has survived and that has every right to be part of the present-day musical scene.

> **They are right to think this way, because for Young rock music is closely connected to life and to human feelings, and the extraordinary and lacerating sound of his guitar bears witness to 40 years of rock music history, and perhaps that of the music of tomorrow.**

> **Supergroup** In 1969 Neil Young, together with David Crosby, Graham Nash, and Stephen Stills, founded the first major "supergroup" in the history of American rock. In this photograph their band is playing in an historic San Francisco venue, Winterland, in 1970.

Gibson Les Paul
Gretsch 6120

< **Live Aid, 1985** Neil Young at JFK Stadium in Philadelphia in 1985, where he played together with Crosby, Stills, and Nash at the massive Live Aid charity concert organized by Bob Geldof.

> **A 1990 performance** Neil Young's guitar playing is extremely personal and creative and his solos are often very long, even interminable, and enervating; but they are never repetitive and predictable, nor are they distorted and noisy in an over-theatrical manner.

>> **Crazy Horse** Neil Young shaking his hair during a 1987 concert. The electric band that has always accompanied Young in these guitar spectacles is Crazy Horse, with which he has recorded his best albums.

> **Progressive rock** Robert Fripp, the heart
and soul of King Crimson, photographed in
London in 1973. The true prince of
progressive rock guitarists, Fripp played his
most famous solo on David Bowie's
"Heroes," which was included on the album
of the same name.

ROBERT FRIPP

Many people have wondered what Robert Fripp did in the G3 trio together with Joe Satriani and Steve Vai. Fripp's virtuosity does not lie in its speed, in the cascades of notes, but rather in its experimentation, in the quest for a potential new sound from his instrument. Vai and Satriani are certainly great guitarists, perhaps a bit too noisy and theatrical, but still highly appreciated guitar heroes of rock. Yet they are light years away from Robert Fripp's innovative, highly curious, and special style. The explanation may lie with the curious, iconoclastic spirit that has always characterized the life and career of one of the best musicians in the entire history of British rock.

The undisputed leader of King Crimson, which was formed in 1968, with a strong, dominating personality, Fripp has also been a guest star with many musicians, including David Bowie, Peter Gabriel, and David Sylvian, since he is able to characterize their work with the unique sound of his instrument and with his style, which took the music of these artists to yet higher levels. Fripp had a much deeper and more innovative relationship with Brian Eno, with whom he invented the "Frippertronics" technique, which radically changed the approach to guitar playing. This consisted of connecting two Revox tape machines on a tape-delay basis, so that the sound of the guitar was recorded on the first machine and then sent on to the second one, and then again played on the first machine and so forth, in a sort of ping-pong, looping procedure in which the sounds continued to overlap and merge while the musician was playing. Thus, Fripp could play by himself in a concert by creating a sound fabric made up of a very intricate pattern of notes. What emerged was an often complex architecture based on stratified musical phrases.

A spin-off of Frippertronics is Soundscapes, in which digital recording provided new possibilities and an infinite range of overlapping sounds, an experiment that Fripp has carried on lately with the League of Crafty Guitarists. In *Circulation,* for example, the guitarists (whose number varies) create amazing arpeggi simply by playing one note each in sequence. With the aid of digital recording machines one can create an intricate counterpoint effect with dozens of voices.

Despite the novelties Fripp injected into guitar playing, the new sound created on David Bowie's *Heroes,* the fruitful collaborations with Eno — especially *(No Pussyfooting)* — the collaboration with David Byrne and Talking Heads, his exploration in jazz with Keith Tippet, in new wave with his wife Toyah Wilcox, the experiments made with Van Der Graaf Generator, Peter Gabriel, Daryl Hall, the Roches, Blondie, and many other bands, despite the decisive role he played in the definition of progressive rock as a bona fide genre, and more in general his contribution to the evolution and development of rock music, despite all this, his best achievements were those with King Crimson. Two masterpieces such as *In the Court of the Krimson King* and *Larks' Tongues in Aspic* are still foundation stones for anyone who wants to say something new in rock music. The very special story of the King Crimson group, the only member of which has remained throughout is Fripp himself, has led this great musician to embark in different directions over the years and to have a formation in which he was not the only guitarist, since he was flanked by another "genius" of this instrument, Adrian Belew. Fripp is also an extraordinary teacher who has created the Guitar Craft course, which he has taught since 1985, giving hundreds of lessons throughout the world.

RORY GALLAGHER

Together with musicians such as Woody Guthrie and Jack Bruce, Rory Gallagher was part of a small group of artists who gave "white blues" the credibility of black blues. In fact, it is always extremely difficult to lend credibility to something, be it art or religion, that does not belong to one's culture. The Irish guitarist was one of those who remained faithful to his style, and his style was a sort of impure blues, because it was tinged with country music but was very effective. It was so American in its Hendrix-type voice and so European in its Cream-like performance. However, there was one thing that was wholly his own and that derived from his measured taste: the total lack of any form of exhibitionism that has led so many other guitarists to use virtuosity for its own sake. His career suffered somewhat because of this.

He was highly regarded by those who love full-blooded blues, but did not enjoy the celebrity heaped on other artists who may have been more forceful but were certainly not so qualified and accomplished. His refusal to replace Mick Taylor in the Rolling Stones reveals how much he rejected contamination and debasement of any kind. Gallagher was not only a master with his Stratocaster, but revealed his skill with acoustic guitars as well, which in his hands sparkled and blazed, especially in the incessant rhythmical changes and convulsive stops of his ragtime.

Having achieved fame with Taste, the legendary band of the first wave of British blues rock that broke up in 1970, Gallagher grew artistically in the 1970s, offering increasingly rich and fascinating music that was linked to the roots of blues but always original, never predictable or obvious. It is no accident that so many guitarists – from The Edge to Slash, Johnny Marr and Brian May – have cited Gallagher as one of their fundamental influences. Rory Gallagher died in 1995.

STEVE HACKETT

The decision made by Steve Hackett when he began to play with Genesis was the same one made by Miles Davis when he became one of the most original musicians of all time: to play only those notes that are necessary. Up to that time (though Robert Fripp had already demolished that convention) virtuosity had been identified with playing a plethora of notes as rapidly as possible: "If you stop worrying about playing fast, you might also be able to come up with new techniques. It's a natural thing... In the future there will always be someone faster than you, and if you really want to be remembered for your music you mustn't concentrate on technique and speed, but on what you want to express."

A painstaking artist, on his debut with Genesis in 1971 (with the album *Nursery Cryme*) Hackett wore large glasses and played while seated, bent over his instrument without looking at anything else except, occasionally, his pedal board – not exactly the typical look of a cool rocker and guitarist. Effects, long notes, and the volume pedal were the distinguishing features of his technique, which allowed him to produce the solo in "Firth of Fifth," which to this day is considered his most successful. On the other hand, his love of classical guitarists and composers, such as J. S. Bach and Barrios, have led to the creation of beautiful works like "Horizons" and "Blood on the Rooftops," in which there is a perfect marriage of sophisticated composition and the sound of the acoustic guitar.

Even before Van Halen, Hackett was the guitarist who lent popularity to tapping, which is the technique used to produce notes by tapping directly on the fret board. He said he discovered the technique because it was the only way to play some triplets by Bach on the guitar.

In the late 1970s the former member of Genesis (he left the group in 1977, after having recorded six studio and two live albums) embarked on a brilliant career as a soloist that was divided equally between classical and rock music, stating that two souls have always coexisted in him, one electric and the other acoustic, and that he loves both modern and old music, which are two marvelous worlds in which one can venture.

< > **Classical and rock** Steve Hackett with his Gibson Les Paul De Luxe during a 1977 concert. After achieving fame as the guitarist of Genesis, with whom he recorded eight albums, Hackett left the band in 1977.

ALEX LIFESON

Alex Lifeson has two faiths, Gibson guitars and the band Rush, the Canadian progressive rock trio that he helped to found, which he has never left and with which he continues to cut albums and go on world tours.

One might say that all his work and musical vision are concentrated on and in Rush, for which he was a virtuoso guitarist in the 1970s, an experimenter with synthesizers and MIDI pedals applied to guitars in the following decade, and again an authentic rocker in the 1990s. Despite all this, Lifeson (whose real family name is Zivojinovich, which in Serbian means literally "son of life") is one of the less famous members of Rush, perhaps due to the lack of special trebles and a true career as a soloist (he cut only one rather insignificant solo album in 1996).

Yet the extreme technical qualities of the band, the maniacal perfection of its music, and the manner in which they manage to re-create live the sound produced in the studio, are for the most part down to Lifeson. Certainly, a trio that makes music such as Rush produces could not continue unless its members were not able to exchange roles and parts. However, all the electronic experimentation that Lifeson carried out in the 1980s now allows him, while playing his guitar, to control with his feet the digital samplers that reproduce the sounds that the trio cannot play individually. These are usually vocal harmonies, accompaniment, and, more in general, "sounds" drawn from studio recordings.

Lifeson began to develop this style and type of sound with such songs as "La Villa Strangiato," "Xanadu," or "YYZ," and not before then. In fact, it was only in 1976, with the album 2112, that the band

achieved the mutual understanding and musical vision that led to their success, which was officially recognized in 1996 when they were made Officers of the Order of Canada – an honor never before conferred to a rock band.

Those who love Rush love Alex Lifeson most of all, his technical prowess, his ability to move into, and experiment with, different musical territories with intelligence, updating techniques and technology over the years, and enlarging the vocabulary of the electric guitar in an exponential manner, transforming it into an instrument that is almost a complete orchestra, in perfect sync with the latest innovations and trends, without ever abandoning the roots of that rock music that changed his life forever when he was 12 years old.

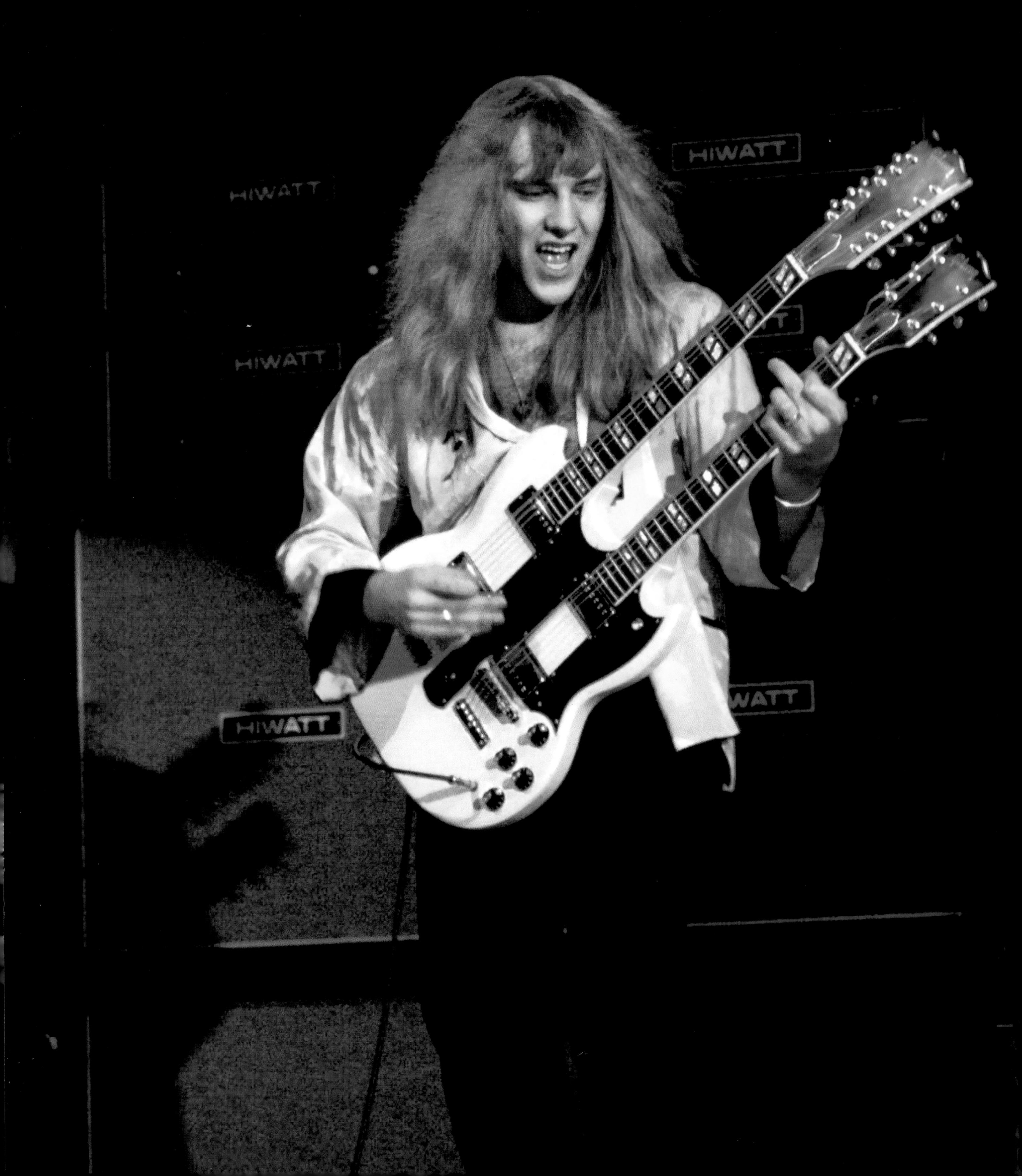
HIWATT
HIWATT
HIWATT
HIWATT

STEVE MORSE

An eclectic personality gifted with a formidable technique, Steve Morse is one of the greatest and most all-around guitar virtuosos of all time. Despite his great skill with jazz, country, classical, and funk, and his equally exceptional ability with both acoustic and electric guitars, Morse had to wait some time before replacing Richie Blackmore in Deep Purple in 1996 (after a stint by Satriani) and gaining great popularity in the world of rock as well. Ian Gilian himself got to know of him only after discovering that he had won the award as the best metal guitarist five times in a row.

Leaving aside his fame, Morse immediately enjoyed success, both as a soloist and with bands he collaborated with in sessions, such as Kansas, thanks to the broad range of his repertoire. Naturally, his musical education and knowledge of musical theory, which he acquired at different schools, places him on a higher level than his colleagues. Before passing on to the rudiments of hard rock, Morse became familiar with musical theory, harmony, and composition, and then with the Dixie Dregs band he went on to create an explosive mixture of rock-fusion. He is an unsurpassed master of alternate picking on the electric guitar, which he executes at breakneck speed.

Besides a Fender Telecaster Custom, for the last 20 years Morse has always played on a Music Man signature model. The readers of *Guitar Player* elected him as the greatest living guitarist, even ahead of Vai and Satriani, and then placed him in the Guitar Player Hall Of Fame.

Morse's career began in the 1960s, when he played with The Plague with his brother Dave, with whom he also performed with The Three. At the Academy of Richmond County he met the bass guitarist Andy West, and the two founded the Dixie Grit band, whose repertoire included covers, and then the Dixie Dregs band. Morse was expelled from the academy and decided to enroll in the Miami School of Music, where Bruce Hornsby, Pat Metheny, Jaco Pastorius, and his friend Andy West also studied in the 1970s. It was with West and other students at Miami that he cut his first album in 1975, *The Great Spectacular*, which was released only two years later.

In 1976 the Dixie Dregs signed a contract with Capricorn and were immediately acclaimed by the critics (however, sales were low) for their its mixture of Southern rock, classical, folk, and country, a fusion that was at once extremely complex yet very enjoyable. When the band broke up the guitarist founded the Steve Morse Band, a trio with Jerry Peek and Doug Morgan. In 1986 Morse joined the Kansas combo, with which he cut two albums. Then came the turning point in his career, when he became part of Deep Purple and his talent was also recognized by the public.

ROBBIE KRIEGER

The classic rock band calls for at least three instruments: guitar, drums, and bass guitar. Who knows what it must have been like for Robbie Krieger to find himself playing in The Doors in which there was no bass but rather a keyboard played by Ray Manzarek. What is more, this was a band which was dominated by its vocalist, Jim Morrison, so much so that the guitarist did not share any of the limelight. So is Krieger only a "sideman"? No, quite the contrary, because not only were Robbie and his guitar decisive factors in the definition of the sound and style of The Doors, but he was also credited with most of the band's success, considering the fact that he wrote such songs as "Light My Fire," "Love Me Two Times," "Touch Me," and "Love Her Madly."

Krieger did not begin as a rock musician. In fact, his first love was flamenco guitar music, whose rules and style he learned by himself. It was around 1963 that things began to change, when he formed a jug band, the Back Bay Chamberpot Terriers, with Bill Wolff. Rock began to circulate in his home city, Los Angeles, together with the new hippy culture, and it was during a lesson on meditation taught by the guru Maharishi Mahesh Yogi that Krieger met the drummer John Densmore and keyboard player Ray Manzarek. He founded a psychedelic band, the Psychedelic Rangers, with Densmore and then, when Manzarek met Morrison and decided to form The Doors, the other two musicians joined the band in 1965. With his highly personal style, his receptiveness to new and different sound, and his great ability as a composer, Krieger has played a major role in the success of the group. And even when he is a frontman, for example with his guitar solos, it is difficult to mistake him for other musicians, because he incorporates jazz and flamenco in his style, displaying a creative aptitude that surpasses his technique by far.

After The Doors broke up, Krieger began to play with different bands, and especially with the Butts Band (with John Densmore) he enjoyed a good deal of success as a jazz guitarist, particularly in the 1980s, while in recent years he has also ventured into the world of fusion.

Gibson Les Paul
Gibson ES 355
Ramirez Flamenco

< **Los Angeles, 1969** Robbie Krieger in December 1969 in Los Angeles, the birthplace of The Doors. A distinguishing feature of this American band was that it had no bass guitar, but consisted of a keyboard player, guitarist, drummer, and vocalist.

> **With the BBC** John Densmore, Jim Morrison, Robbie Krieger, and Ray Manzarek, that is to say, The Doors, photographed in 1968 at the zenith of the band's success, playing on the BBC program *Top of the Pops*.

< **I Am a Bluesman** Among the greats of American blues rock guitarists, a place of honor must go to Johnny Winter. A legend of Texan music who from the 1960s on, often together with his brother Edgar, has produced a handful of excellent recordings despite a great many personal problems. One of the albums was recorded in the late 1970s, when Winter played with the great Muddy Waters.

JOHNNY WINTER

No one is an exception to the rule that "blues are for black folks" more than Johnny Winter, who has been an authentic bluesman since he was 15 years old. Like all his peers, he began early and played with bands at school and was able to see live performances of such blues legends as B.B. King, Muddy Waters, and Bobby Bland in the 1950s, when they were at the peak of their careers.

A major breakthrough came about only in 1968, when he was the leader of a trio (guitar, bass guitar, and drums) and an article about him appeared in *Rolling Stone* that triggered interest in his playing and led to contacts and fame. Consequently, Winter was able to cut his first album, whose title bears his name, and he played at Woodstock. The fact that he did not appear in Wadleigh's film of the festival stopped him from becoming a legendary figure then and there, as occurred with other musicians who participated in the festival.

Despite this, Winter's fame grew rapidly, reaching its height in terms of album sales in 1971 with *Live/Johnny Winter And,* a spare and typical live recording that anticipated the tendency of all his production in the 1970s, which was oriented much more to blues rather than to rock.

It may be that his devotion to the roots of black music (whose history has always been brimful of stories and anecdotes that verge on the improbable) has made him the subject of many urban legends. The most famous one (which Winter has denied on many an occasions, though in vain) has it that he performed with Jimi Hendrix and Jim Morrison that eventful evening when the two performed together on stage.

After appearing on the cover of the first issue of *Guitar World* in 1980, Winter entered the Blues Foundation Hall Of Fame in 1988. He always idolized Muddy Waters, and even had the privilege of playing with him on his last two albums, *Hard Again and King Bee,* which earned him various Grammy Awards.

To this day, although he admits to playing and preferring "old-fashioned" music, Johnny Winter refuses to be labeled as a rock musician, and proved this in 2004 with his last album after eight years of silence entitled *I Am a Bluesman.*

STEVE HOWE

While it true to say that the great majority of rock guitarists learned to play by themselves, it is equally true that not all of them developed such a magnificent technique as Steve Howe's. From the outset, his introverted character led him to study a great deal by himself and to take into consideration all the aspects and potential of his instrument. This is why both with the band Yes and by himself Howe has created significant acoustic pieces (such as the two great classics "Clap" and "Mood For a Day") as well as electric guitar solos that are full of creativity and absolutely explosive.

In the late 1960s, Steve made significant contributions in sessions first with the Tomorrow and then with the Bodast bands, but these experiences turned out to be great disappointments. In vain he auditioned for Atomic Rooster and Jethro Tull, and he even played (for only one evening) with the Nice: "An evening with Nice is an evening too many" Keith Emerson once stated.

Howe joined Yes in 1970. If in the *The Yes Album* his sound is different from the preceding recordings of this band and can be considered among the masterpieces of progressive rock, it was precisely thanks to the new guitarist that the group attained extraordinary versatility. From blues to jazz, from ragtime to Hendrix's rock, with his superb technique – whether pure (that is, adopting either fingerpicking or the pick) or hybrid (utilizing the fingers and pick together) – Howe is a truly all-around guitarist, both when he plays his Gibson or his Martin, the only two guitars he has always used (despite the fact that over the years he has become a fanatical collector of stringed instruments). His search for an ever different sound and timbre is not limited to using different guitars, but has included experiments with the mandolin, the sitar, the koto, and various other instruments (including even the harp), which are usually adopted in pop music in a very unoriginal manner.

Leaving aside a brief interval in the 1980s, Howe has always played with Yes, while at the same time continuing to cultivate his career as a soloist, as a member of Asia (its first two albums), the GTR group (together with Steve Hackett), and various sessions – the most famous of which is the one with Queen, for which he wrote and played the flamenco guitar solo of *Innuendo*.

BRUCE SPRINGSTEEN

The exuberance of rock in the 1950s combined with the profundity of the 1960s and molded for the 1970s; this is the impression made by the sound of Bruce Springsteen during the period of his first great hit, *Born To Run.* This album, after years of relative obscurity marked by trials and experimentation with his E Street Band, launched him into the status of the great white hope of American rock and on to legendary stardom.

Further proof of his greatness came with the various tours he made in the following years. In fact, the best expression of Springsteen's music is to be found in his live performances, very long concerts that are a perfect blend of ballads, rock hymns, and lyrics relating ordinary life fraught with difficulties that can win over even the most skeptical opponent of rock.

Springsteen is the interpreter of what has been called heartland rock, the white rock music of New Jersey that is directly linked to southern rock and country music. With his own,

unique poetic quality, he focuses on the lower classes and blue-collar workers, on difficult relationships, on the daily struggle to stay afloat in the hope of finding happiness, on the condition of war veterans, and on a series of other themes based on grass roots American culture – that body of traditions and values that grew up in the eastern United States in the early 20th century.

However, the fundamental moment of his career and his music is still the period from 1975 to 1987, that is, from *Born To Run* to *Tunnel Of Love,* a period marked by one huge success after the other, highly acclaimed and popular tours, and incredible fame for The Boss (the nickname the other members of the E Street Band gave him because he was the one who always collected their fees at their gigs and then doled out the money).

It was precisely in this period that his fans established certain stereotypes that he has never succeeded in shedding. But in reality The Boss is much more versatile than this, able to pass from such highly successful commercial hits as the double *The River* to more difficult and

introspective albums, such as *Nebraska* (the pioneer work of lo-fi sound), from pop to the very recent *Working on a Dream* and the spectacular folk qualities of *We Shall Overcome: The Seeger Sessions.* Springsteen has always alternated these two types of works and has always managed to keep the critics on his side and to win back the fans he had lost either because of his contemplative vein or ventures into pop, remaining faithful only to his electric and acoustic guitars, the inseparable companions of his amazing and passionate musical adventure.

Springsteen is a rock guitarist in the most classic and most profound sense of the term, a musician who travels and dreams with his guitar, runs off and then returns to build anew in solos that first strike your heart intensely and then stirs your mind. His guitar technique is never spectacular, but his poetic expressivity is truly magnificent and the combination of the two makes him one of rock's greatest guitarists.

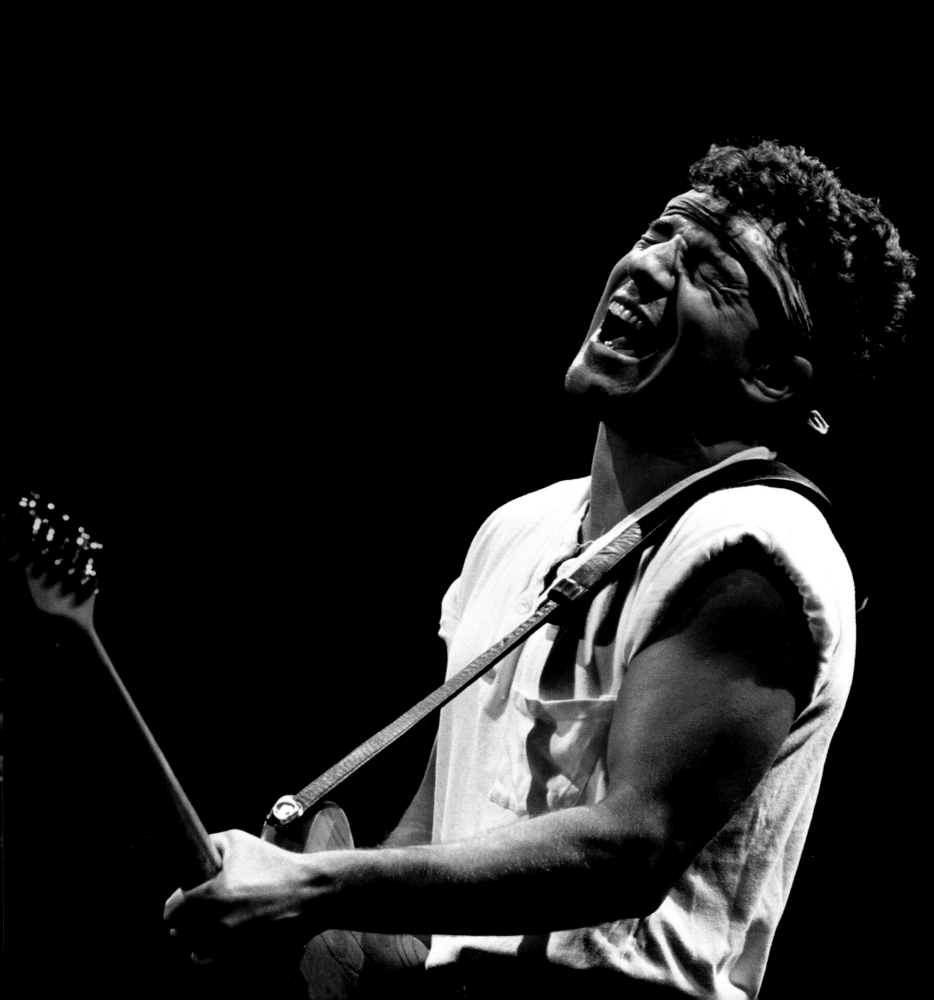

Preceding pages

< **Composer and soloist** Most of Bruce Springsteen's success and image has been based on the idea of breaking down all walls and boundaries with his electric guitar. He is not only an excellent composer, but also a first-rate soloist.

> **Superstar in 1985** Springsteen achieved his greatest success in the mid-1980s with *Born in the U.S.A.*, an album that launched him into stardom. But being a superstar did not mean betraying and abandoning his rock roots.

< > **Human Rights Now** In the autumn of 1988, Bruce Springsteen, Youssou N'Dour, Sting, Peter Gabriel, and Tracy Chapman participated in the Human Rights Now world tour. Here we see the Boss on stage in New Delhi, September 30, 1988.

Following pages

< **The maestro of live performances** Springsteen and the E Street Band supported the Amnesty International campaign with the Human Rights Now tour in 1988. The finale of these performances consisted of Springsteen and the other artists singing "Chimes of Freedom."

> **Electric and acoustic** In his live performances, Springsteen is only too happy to play the electric guitar in the more impactive pieces, while he often uses the acoustic guitar in new versions of his most famous songs.

Fender Esquire
Fender Telecaster

JOE SATRIANI

Few guitarists have a resumé to equal that of the Italian-American Joe Satriani. He began playing at the age of 14 and wh
e was 20 he was already teaching guitar (some of his most famous pupils include Steve Vai, Kirk Hammett, and Charlie Hun
mong others).

When Mick Jagger decided to play without the Rolling Stones and without Keith Richards, he asked Satriani to perform with him. When Deep Purple needed a great guitarist, they called on him.

Satriani has cut numerous gold and platinum records (including such memorable albums as *Surfing with the Alien* and *Th
xtremist*). When asked "Who is the best guitarist in the world?" an entire generation replied in unison: "Joe Satriani". He al
rmed the G3 concert tour project, in which he played with other legendary guitarists, inlcuding Robert Fripp, Steve Vai, and
ngwie Malmsteen. In short, Satriani has been and is one of the most popular guitarists in the world, highly appreciated by h
olleagues, loved by the public, gifted with amazing technique, often able to come up with major breakthroughs, and capable
combining various genres and styles with his great technical prowess and superb agility. This virtuosity may have
vershadowed his persona, but it has allowed him to enter the new millennium in splendid form and to continue to produce
variably successful music.

Satriani came onto the scene in the mid-1980s with his first album and was immediately considered a true "guitar hero"
the public. Success arrived with his second album *Surfing with the Alien,* which paved the way to stardom. He can play jus
out anything, from jazz to blues, from fusion to rock, funk and reggae – his music clearly exhibits the influence of all these
nres – and also electronic and dance music. Gifted with incomparable technical prowess, Satriani is also a first-rate melodi
aving written both romantic ballads and explosive compositions. He is a great innovator of guitar technique, as well as an
ntiring explorer of new sounds, which has made it possible for him to play with musicians with highly different styles. His
test adventure has been with a new band consisting of Chad Smith of Red Hot Chili Peppers, Sammy Hagar, and Michael
nthony from Van Halen. However, this will certainly not be the last stage of his career, because Satriani breathes music ar
s guitar is never at rest.

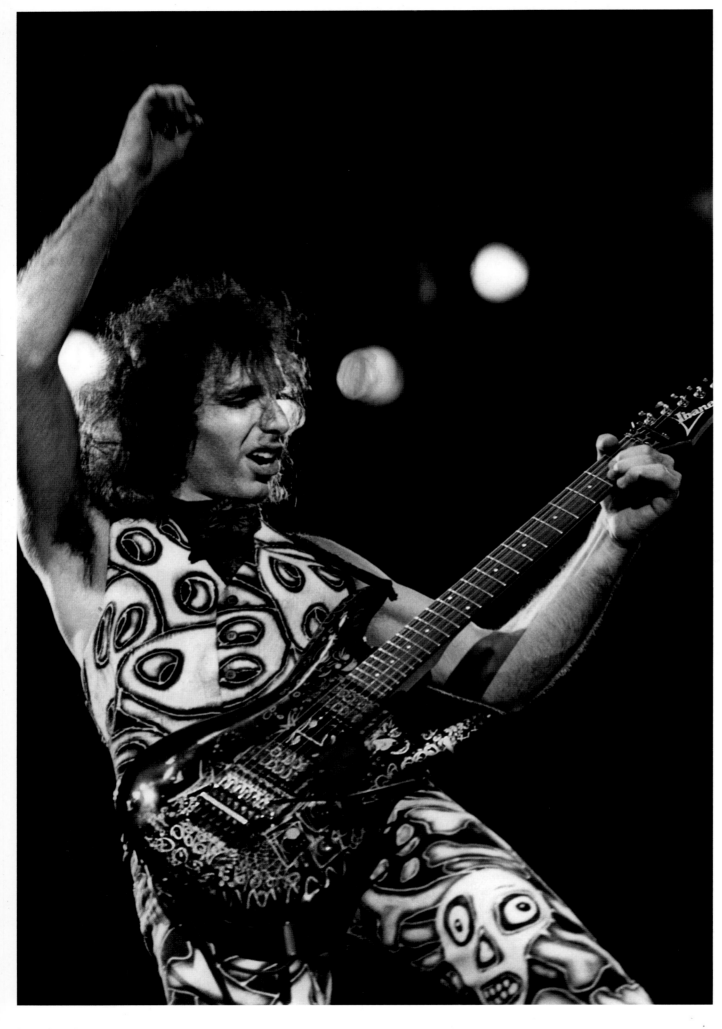

< One of the most popular Jazz, blues, hard rock, fusion, and pop: there is no genre that Satriani has not played with success, becoming one of the favorites among fans of guitar playing.

> Bone Bash Tour, 2002 Joe Satriani performing at the Chronicle Pavilion in Concord, California, during his 2002 Bone Bash Tour. The guitarist also played with Mick Jagger during the latter's first tour without the Rolling Stones.

Ibanez JS

ANDY SUMMERS

This English guitarist auditioned as a replacement for Mick Taylor as lead guitarist of the Rolling Stones (the audition was "won" by Ron Wood). He could have been the lead for Soft Machine (he played for a short time with this group but never recorded with them) and he also recorded sessions with Neil Sedaka, Jon Lord, Kevin Ayers, Kevin Coyne, Zoot Money, and Eric Burdon and The New Animals. But Andy Summers (originally known as Andy Somers) was the guitarist of one of the most powerful rock music trios, The Police, from 1979 until the group broke up, and then again when the three musicians recently reunited. Together with the American Stewart Copeland and the Englishman Sting, Andy Summers with his acid, syncopated, and sometimes psychedelic sound made a fundamental contribution to

the creation of the burgeoning new wave sound.

Usually taking a back seat, so to speak, when compared to the creative importance of Sting and the determined, powerful technique of Stewart Copeland, Summers deserves credit for having been a fundamental element in the creation of a new musical style that combined the rediscovery of the origins of rock on the part of the punk movement and the heavy rhythm of the reggae tradition.

Despite the fact that in his career he has alternated rock with soundtrack production for films and with various essays in fusion and jazz, especially after The Police broke up, Andy Summers's special sound has always been identified with the Fender Telecaster he played with The Police in the basic guitar passages of such songs as "Message in a Bottle," "Don't Stand So Close to Me," and "Every Breath You Take," and with the use he has made of the tape-delay machine, chorus, compressor, and echo to

create new effects, creating an absolutely original style in a period in the history of rock in which the role played by the electric guitar was seriously jeopardized by the rise of the electronic keyboard. Summers is not a star guitarist, but of the three members of The Police he is the one with the richest and most varied musical culture and experience, much of which is based on a thorough knowledge of jazz. And it is precisely jazz that Summers turned to after the break up of The Police, playing with different combos, without neglecting his passion for experimentation (together with Robert Fripp), for new age music, and for movie soundtracks. Summers was one of the great innovators of electric guitar rock in the late 1970s, and his style has influenced dozens of guitarists of later generations.

Fender Telecaster
Fender Stratocaster
Gibson ES 335

< **From Punk to New Wave** Andy Summers on stage with The Police in 1979. The band was formed during the heyday of punk music, but it soon became a part of the new wave trend, precisely because of Summers's different approach to guitar playing.

> **Acid and syncopated sound** Andy Summers has had an extremely close relationship with The Police. When the band broke up he made soundtracks and realized interesting projects, but without attaining the success he had had with Sting and Copeland.

JOHNNY RAMONE

Johnny Ramone's real name was John William Cummings, but everyone in the world knew him as Johnny Ramone, the guitarist of the American punk band The Ramones. This New Yorker from Long Island founded the band along with Joey, Tommy, and Dee Dee, and for 22 years his truly unmistakable sound was the Ramones' trademark. Johnny's is the classic rock 'n' roll biography: a difficult adolescence with some minor problems with the law and drugs, a life doomed to have no future that was saved by his passion for rock. Johnny loved the Stooges and Mc5, and in the early 1970s founded his first band,

Tangerine Puppets, which included Tommy Ramone. But it was meeting Dee Dee that proved to be decisive. They had a common passion for music, which they talked about constantly. In 1974, after going out to buy some instruments, they decided to form The Ramones. This was when punk was still far away, but the Ramones formula was seminal: extremely fast pieces with only a few chords, two minutes at most, and bang! that was that. The Ramones went on stage in the mid-1970s and in a short time they became the leading band on the New York scene and then went on to revolutionize the entire American rock world. This was the band that led a generation of young English musicians to create punk rock. It was they who in such New York clubs as CbGb's and Max's Kansas City were catalysts for burgeoning new wave music. They never had outstanding sales, but they were one of the most influential bands in the history of rock.

Johnny had a fast and energetic style that soon became the style of American new wave guitarists, consisting of barré chords that were down-stroked rapidly, often following a I-IV-V progression, a technique that became very popular, especially among such English heavy metal bands as Iron Maiden and Judas Priest, and even more popular during the emergence of grunge rock. Johnny was basically a first-rate rhythmic guitarist gifted with such taste and expressive power that listeners hardly ever noticed the almost total absence of virtuosity or felt the need for solos. This was why his influence on the American music scene of the 1980s and 1990s was so enormous, in terms of both sound and image, giving rise to an entire generation of rhythmical guitarists who took their cue from his style and then pushed it on farther. His appearance, which was derived from the aesthetic rebellion of the 1950s – long straight hair covering most of his face, a leather jacket he never took off, with a white T-shirt underneath it, his guitar strap so long that he held the instrument almost at knee level – became a standard model for modern rock as well. Even his guitar, a white Mosrite Ventures II Model, became an icon.

Despite the "rebellious music" of the Ramones, Johnny was an easygoing person, a Republican in political matters, faithful to his wife (who was Joey's former girlfriend, which is the reason why the two never spoke to each other afterwards), and entirely devoted to his guitar and to rock 'n' roll, of which he was one of the leading modern interpreters.

Mosrite Ventures II

> **London, 1979** Johnny Ramone and the Ramones on stage at the Hammersmith Odeon in London at the peak of the English punk explosion in 1979. That tour marked the beginning of the American band's success in Europe.

Following pages

< **Superfast style** Johnny, Tommy, and Joey Ramone during a concert held in 1977. The nightclub where their band became known, along with so many other top American rock groups, was CBGB's in New York City, which recently had to shut down.

> **Original rock'n'roll** Johnny Ramone performing in 1980. The band was associated with the American punk style, but its roots lay in rock 'n' roll, which it interpreted in a truly original and highly modern fashion.

Ramones

I hate the teachers and the principal.
Dont wanna be taught to be no fool.
Rock, rock, rock, rock, rock'n'roll high school
(1979 - Rock'n'Roll High School)

< > **CBGB's, 1976** Johnny Ramone, Joey Ramone, and Dee Dee Ramone playing at CBGB's in 1976, at the beginning of their extraordinary musical career. Patti Smith, Talking Heads, and Blondie often performed at this club.

PRINCE

"Get Dirty At the club were in
Use it around your waist like a
chain within
I got that call so I jumped in my car
I love you baby
But not like I Love my Guitar"

These lines from the song
"Guitar" emphatically demonstrate
the relationship between Prince
Roger Nelson and his guitar – a
close, deep, and physical
relationship, around which he has
constructed his prodigious musical
career. Without a doubt Prince is
the most important African-
American guitarist after Jimi
Hendrix, yet he is another of those
musicians whose fame as an
entertainer and vocalist have
obscured his merits as a guitarist.
How can this be? Personalities
such as Prince, who are so
exposed to the mass media, often

run this risk, even knowingly. And
certainly Prince has deliberately
faced risks to the hilt, because all
things considered his multi-faceted
gifts as an entertainer dominate
the guitarist in him.

However, if we limit these
considerations to music, the
comparison with Hendrix is only
partly true, if only because
Prince's relationship with funky
music and rhythm 'n' blues is
much more profound than the one
Hendrix had with the same
genres. And it must also be said
that rock is only one of the
components of Prince's musical
universe, and not its fundamental
element. But then Prince shares
Hendrix's love for
experimentation, for surpassing
limits and, above all, his
extremely close rapport with his
guitar, which he views as a sexual
object, a means of communication,
a partner, a ritual element. Like
Hendrix, Prince has revived the
central role played by the guitar
in the development of black music,
emancipating it from the function
of mere rhythmical

accompaniment as imposed by
soul music and to a lesser degree
by funk.

Prince's approach to playing
the guitar is instinctive, as can
be seen in his shows and his most
important hits, particularly
"Purple Rain" (the film of the
same name won the 1984 Oscar
for best original song score) and
"Kiss," which both feature superb
guitar elements. The first makes
exaggerated use of the flanger,
thus making it immediately
recognizable; the second has a
pressing stop-and-go rhythm and
beat. However, Prince's guitar can
also shout, as in "Peach."

In 1978 he released the album
For You, which demonstrated his
skills as a multi-instrumentalist
and which he also produced and
cut by himself, so earning the title
of the new Stevie Wonder (Prince
has stated that Wonder was the
person who influenced him most).
But he became a world-famous
star with *Purple Rain,* both due
to the album and the film it was
scored for. Up to the 1990s the
Minneapolis musician dominated

the musical scene, competing with
the great stars of that period
(Madonna, Michael Jackson,
Springsteen, and U2) in stadiums
and other venues throughout the
world, stringing together a long
series of successes as a composer,
singer, dancer, and actor. Then
came his rebellion against the
rules of the record companies and
certain dramatic personal events
that sent him into a long period
of crisis, from which he emerged,
once again with success, into the
new millennium.

Prince has been and still is
one of the most fascinating
personalities of popular music.
A guitarist with great technique
and expression, a musician whose
versatility and all-around
excellence led Miles Davis to call
him – with a bit of exaggeration –
the new Duke Ellington.

> I never wanted 2 be your weekend lover
I only wanted 2 be some kind of friend
Baby I could never steal u from another
It's such a shame our friendship had 2 end.

Purple rain purple rain . . .

(1984 - Purple Rain)

< **Composer and musician** Prince has managed a fascinating crossover between different genres, especially funk, as well as soul, rock, and pop, which he is very familiar with both as a composer and musician.

> **Prince Roger Nelson** Prince in a 1985 concert in Detroit, Michigan. This guitarist reached the peak of his success in the 1980s. A multi-instrumentalist and vocalist, Prince Roger Nelson has always used the electric guitar as his main instrument.

DAVE MUSTAINE

A handful of modern guitarists have rapidly achieved legendary status and certainly one of them is Dave Mustaine. As a guitarist, vocalist, and leader of Megadeth he has become one of the major stars of thrash metal.

After a difficult childhood, Mustaine discovered the world of music with the aid of his sister, rock, and through the persona and music of Alice Cooper ("my godfather" as he once said). Obviously, the rock that Mustaine loved was the hardest, electric variety as played by Motörhead, Black Sabbath, Iron Maiden, and AC/DC. Hard rock and heavy metal were his musical points of reference. Mustaine rapidly acquired a fine technique and passion, and at the age of 16 he was already considered one of the best metal talents in Los Angeles. In 1981, after answering an ad in a local newspaper, he auditioned for a new band looking for a lead guitarist. The members listened to him and immediately asked him to join: this was how Dave Mustaine became one of the members of Metallica. However, this experience lasted only two years, as the band ordered him to leave in 1983 because of his serious drug and alcohol problems and his increasing squabbles with Lars Ulrich and James Hetfield. Word has it that the tension was particularly strong between Hetfield and Mustaine, and in fact both later stated in public that there never had been feeling and understanding between them.

However, Mustaine did not give up and after a brief spell with Fallen Angel he formed his own band, Megadeth, which fans consider ranks alongside Metallica, Slayer, and Anthrax as one of the most important thrash metal bands.

Dave Mustaine is the undisputed leader and the only remaining member of the original group. The band changed its musical style several times over the years, passing from the thrash metal it began with to a melodic heavy metal and then, for a brief period, to a type of hard rock with an industrial slant, but in recent years it has revived elements of its original thrash sound. The changes always coincided with those made in Metallica. Indeed, for his entire career Mustaine has felt the need to compete with his former colleagues in a curious and yet very stimulating musical competition in which the best achievements in creativity alternated between the two bands.

Fast and noisy Dave Mustaine playing with Megadeth at the Download Festival, Donington Park, UK in 2007. Mustaine is known not only for his extremely fast and noisy style, but also for his gift as a composer.

Dean VMNT
ESP
Jackson Y2KV
Gibson Flying V

MICHAEL
SCHENKER

There are not many people on the German rock music scene who have managed to achieve international success and fame. In fact, those that have can be counted on the fingers of one hand and none has had more success than Michael Schenker. He achieved success in the crowded world of heavy metal as the leader of such famous bands as Scorpions, UFO, and the Michael Schenker Group. For lovers of heavy metal guitar playing, Schenker is a legend and considered a great innovator who has influenced generations of guitarists.

According to heavy metal tradition, Schenker began playing the guitar at an early age when his brother Rudolf gave him a Gibson Flying V guitar for his birthday. Michael, who was only nine years old at the time, began to play the instrument and to learn the most popular songs of the time. He fell in love with the Beatles, then with hard rock, memorized the solos of Eric Clapton and Jimmy Page, and then turned to the new hard rock of Tony Iommi and Black Sabbath and the electric blend of Richie Blackmore and Deep Purple. He was only 11 when he formed his first band, the Enervates, 15 when his brother Rudolf decided to found Scorpions, and only 16 when the band cut and released its first album. Soon afterward, Schenker joined the English band UFO, becoming its main composer and enjoying success throughout Europe. However, his UFO experience was somewhat turbulent; Schenker's behavior was erratic, which brought about serious problems with the other members of the band. He eventually left UFO in 1978 and resumed playing with his brother and Scorpions for a

few months. After an audition with Black Sabbath the restless Michael decided to have nothing more to do with other bands and that the moment had arrived to go it alone. In 1979 he founded the Michael Schenker Group, a band without any permanent members that relied on musicians stepping in according to Schenker's requirements and projects at any particular time. With this band he has enjoyed 25 years of success (although he has often performed again with UFO), alternating fruitful phases with periods of depression and rather poor musical results.

GEORGE THOROGOOD

< > **Powerful rock blues** George Thorogood in a photograph taken in 1970. He hails from Wilmington, Delaware and is one of the most powerful blues rock guitarists around. His song "Bad to the Bone" enhances one of the classic scenes in *Terminator*.

If you are a true lover of rock blues you must absolutely have a record featuring George Thorogood and The Destroyers. He made his debut in the 1970s and from the end of that decade to the early 1980s, with *Move It On Over and Bad to the Bone,* Thorogood achieved success and was recognized as one of the leading exponents of this musical genre. Everything Thorogood does conforms precisely to the rules of rock blues and his devotion to the genre and the constant certainty of being in the right without allowing himself to be "corrupted" by trends or innovations have led to a continuous increase in the number of his fans.

Thorogood's first album dates to 1977 and was a record that, despite the explosion of punk from the Pacific to the Atlantic, immediately brought this young American guitarist to the attention of the public for his genuine and precise style. His riffs are memorable (how can one forget the one in "Bad to the Bone" in *Teminator II?*), his guitar style is solid, rugged, and passionate, there is not one note out of place in his solos, and everything is exactly as it should be in a good blues album. Immune to trends and fashions, Thorogood never disappoints his public, especially in his live concerts, and continues to provide electrifying and overwhelming shows.

ADRIAN BELEW

In whatever recording he was involved with, Adrian Belew was always considered a guest of honor. From Zappa to Bowie, Tori Amos and the recent recordings made by Nine Inch Nails, Belew always gave a fine performance and left a highly personal stamp on his work – even at the "royal courts" of stars who did not relish the idea of sharing the spotlight. A perfect case in point is that of King Crimson. Robert Fripp was certainly not the kind of person who would allow anyone to have the role of joint lead guitarist in his group. But with Belew and three recordings – *Discipline, Beat,* and *Three of a Perfect Pair* – two things occurred: the singer was not necessarily the bass player (as was the case with Wetton and Lake), because Belew also has a fine voice; and the new sound, which was usually invented by Fripp,

this time came from the other guitarist. In fact, Belew's sound is absolutely indefinable because it is always different, it is what makes *Remain in Light* by the Talking Heads so extraordinary. It is pioneering, referring to the past and the future at the same time, and extremely varied. The unorthodox methods in his use of effects and of the tremolo bar (Belew has always been faithful to his Strato guitar) are what make his renditions so original.

An emblematic example of his experimentation is "Animal Kingdom" (from the album *Coming Attractions*), in which Belew uses a Fender Stratocaster, which was obviously modified, to imitate the sounds animals make. If the comparison did not seem to be difficult in terms of sound classification, one would go so far as to say that Belew is a profoundly "Hendrixian" guitarist, interested in technique only to a degree and amazingly enamored of sound, or sounds, and of the original

sound potential of his guitar. This is a characteristic of his that has allowed him to work with dozens of different bands and musicians over the years without ever becoming a bandleader. An American from Kentucky, Belew became known to the rock public when he played together with Frank Zappa (which says quite a lot about his musical gifts), and it was during the 1978 tour with Zappa that he was noticed by David Bowie, who immediately asked Belew to work with him. Through Bowie he met Fripp and Eno, and then the Talking Heads, which marked the beginning of an extraordinary career made up of solo albums that never enjoyed great success and of work with artists that range from Paul Simon to Nine Inch Nails. Without a doubt, Belew can be considered one of the great innovators of modern guitar playing.

Fender Stratocaster
Roland Guitar Synthesizer

MARK KNOPFLER

It was a truly courageous feat for Mark Knopfler and Dire Straits to challenge punk music during its heyday. The refinement of this Scottish guitarist has nothing at all to do with the crude – albeit effective – songs that were the rage in England in the late 1970s. However, it must be said that the first album he cut with his band, with the signature single of the entire output of Dire Straits, "Sultans of Swing," was in perfect sync with the simple, minimal, and direct aesthetic of new wave music, which rejected frills and useless display and was in opposition to the baroque sound of progressive music. It is precisely this curious

combination of tradition and modernity that makes Knopfler's contribution to the history of the rock guitar so unique.

Knopfler's style, while not unique, is rather original for a rock guitarist, and above all it differs from the style of those who play on the Fender Stratocaster (his favorite along with the Schecter). He never uses a pick but plays only with his fingers, and not even all of them. In general he places the forefinger and ring finger on the body and makes tiny movements with the other three. The sounds that emerge are crisp, clear and brilliant, partly because he uses effects moderately, if at all, which contributes to the distinction of the individual notes even in fast passages. His solos have a lyrical quality that is the distinguishing feature of his style, which obviously derives from the first instrument he played, the violin. Blending, even on two strings, and legato are the features of a

character this is often foreign to rock and closer to the feeling and approach of jazz music. In fact, Knopfler is one of the guitarists who has established a particular mode of playing that has influenced and inspired many guitarists. Yet it was precisely the period in which he came to the fore that makes his career and music even more important. In a phase of rock when both the guitar soloist and, in general, the guitar were "banished" from the scene, first with punk and then with electronic new wave, Knopfler succeeded in finding a niche for his instrument, and not with a nostalgic public but with an entirely new generation of fans, which allowed the guitar to continue to be a major and popular instrument.

Mark Knopfler made famous the Dobro guitar, which was used on "Romeo and Juliet" and illustrated on the cover of the *Brothers in Arms* album. Recently, a new Strato model was named

after him. His career has remained hand in glove with the Dire Straits group, despite the fact that as a soloist he has recorded interesting and beautiful pieces, is the author of soundtracks, and has played with the legendary Chet Atkins, Bob Dylan, Sting, Eric Clapton, John Fogerty, Steely Dan, Phil Lynott, Tina Turner, Van Morrison, and Randy Newman, who specifically asked him to accompany them because his sound is unmistakable, so characteristic, able to create such special, absolutely extraordinary atmospheres. In short, Knopfler was one of the leading guitarists of the late 20th century.

Fender Stratocaster
Gibson Les Paul
Martin Dreadnought

< Rock, country, blues and pop Knopfler's points of reference have always wavered between England and the United States, including rock, country, and blues, as well as melody and pop. He has achieved a harmonious balance of this influences in his music that has proved to be extremely popular.

> Producer After Dire Straits broke up, Knopfler continued to produce very interesting albums and soundtracks, and also made several tours that were well received. He also improved his guitar playing, becoming one of the best soloists in the world.

Following pages

< > An alternative to new wave Dire Straits during a concert performed in 1993. The English combo came up with an interesting alternative to new wave and electronic in the middle of the 1980s that was very popular.

STEVE VAI

Very few have had the privilege of being taught to play the guitar by Joe Satriani and also being a pupil of Frank Zappa. Steve Vai, however, is just such a person when at the tender age of 18, after years of hard practice, he decided to send Frank Zappa a cassette with some of his recordings and his own arrangement of "The Black Page." His transcription of this impossible piece and his guitar playing so impressed Zappa that he signed Vai up immediately as his transcriber. Naturally, this rather humble position was not fit for such a talent as the young Vai possessed, and only two years later he was recording guitar parts on some of the many Zappa albums (including the famous duet in "Sofa" that earned him a Grammy Award in 1994) and he performed with Zappa during his endless tours.

The distinguishing features of Vai's future greatness were already becoming apparent: great virtuoso technique, total control of his instrument, and creative exploration of the various potential dimensions of the guitar sound. The difficult years working with and for Zappa, who would remain his source of inspiration and reference point, served to improve his already great technique even more, a technique that came to the fore in his first solo album, *Flex-Able* (1984). However, the album did not sell well, which forced Vai to continue as a session guitarist. Fortunately, this "supporting role" work increased in quality and importance. The turning point came in 1990 with the release of *Passion and Warfare*, one of the most important and interesting virtuoso rock albums of the 1980s.

Humor, great technique, and the exploration of all the possible sounds and dimensions of the electric guitar are the main features of Vai's style, which in the studio emerges in complex webs and live on stage explodes in a dynamic and frenzied performance spiced with continuous changes of clothes and guitars, all of which are Ibanez, such as his signature model JEM, which has the neck incorporated into the body, a mother-of-pearl plectrum, and a Tree of Life inlay on the neck.

One might not love his music and some may accuse him of wasting his incredible talent on producing music that is highly spectacular but low in quality, but one cannot but love Steven Vai and his guitar, his acrobatic way of playing, the amazing, even unthinkable, number of notes he manages to fit into a single solo. He is a true "guitar hero," a genius who delights in using (if not squandering) his awesome gifts in pop music and the circus of virtuoso performances. Vai is certainly one of the few modern guitarists who can compete with the greats of the past, one of the very few of those who can be placed in the pantheon of the all-time giants of the rock guitar.

< **Session Man** Steve Vai performing at Shepherds Bush Empire, London in 1997. Vai has played in several bands, including Alcatrazz and Whitesnake, and to this day he often plays with G3, along with Joe Satriani.

> **An untiring experimenter** Steve Vai playing at Melkweg, one of the most famous rock clubs in Amsterdam, July 18, 2007. An untiring experimenter with new techniques, he is famous above all for his unsurpassed tapping.

Ibanez Jem
Ibanez Edge
Ibanez Universe (a seven-string guitar)

‹ › A producer of records as well as honey
Steve Vai in a live performance in 2002. He has
cut many records together with international
pop artists. Vai is a highly appreciated producer
of records as well as of honey "The fire garden
honey."

STEVIE RAY VAUGHAN

Having inherited a grand tradition, Stevie Ray Vaughan was the last great personification of the typical American bluesman, a fine musician whose career was under a curse: five albums in seven years of activity (from 1983 to 1990), and then an untimely death in a helicopter accident (which he decided to fly in at the last moment instead of taking a bus to Chicago). Besides his official releases there is also an endless series of collaborations with the best blues musicians of the 1980s, giants such as Albert King, who was also one of Vaughan's idols.

A revolutionary, modern, and innovative musician the likes of which had not been seen for some time in the world of blues rock, Stevie Ray Vaughan, just like another of his idols, Jimi Hendrix, had a style distinguished by the particular manner in which he succeeded in covering the rhythmical accompaniment and the solo parts at the same time, with a special sound that he created with his guitar, which was almost always a Fender, by using thick and heavy strings and lowering the tuning by a half note.

He was noticed in 1982 by David Bowie and Jackson Browne during the Montreux Jazz Festival together with his band, Double Trouble. Vaughan was immediately signed up by the former for his album *Let's Dance* and for the tour that followed, in which the bluesman did not take part, however. Like all self-respecting blues musicians, he methodically and constantly cultivated self-destruction. Drug and alcohol abuse led to several crises and seizures, until a particularly severe attack during a European tour in 1986 forced Stevie Ray to decide to play only three more performances and then seek help from Dr. Victor Bloom, who was well known for already having helped Eric Clapton and Pete Townshend. The doctor told Vaughan that if he had not come to the hospital he would have died within a month. The bluesman miraculously managed to achieve total rehabilitation by himself only in 1990, the year of his tragic accident.

THE EDGE

> **A great innovator** The Edge performing in San Diego during U2's 2005 Vertigo Tour. The Irish musician was one of the leading innovators of new wave guitar playing in the 1980s.

The return to the most authentic, sincere, and intimate "rock" dimension of pop music took place in the second half of the 1980s thanks to U2. The distinctive sound of this band is mostly due to the guitar and echo effect of The Edge.

In fact, for David Howell Evans the echo pedal and reverb effects that one can create with the guitar are a true instrument in themselves, as much as the six strings that this musician admits he uses very little. The Edge calls notes "expensive," which is why he tries to use them as little as possible, shaping a world of sound based on echoes. However, the original idea of using these effects was not his, but was suggested to him by his friend Bono, who cited as a good example the beginning of the Pink Floyd's album *Animals*. Likewise, his nickname The Edge was not his idea, but was given by others due to his mania for walking on the edge of high walls and for his angular facial features.

The Edge has always been faithful to his Gibson guitars, usually Les Paul, which is the only constant in his rock persona, since over the years he has changed his look several times, ranging from a "long-hair" appearance in the 1980s to a totally shaven head covered by a skullcap in recent years.

The Edge wsa one of the founders of U2 along with his brother, who left the group in 1978. While it is true that Bono, the frontman and leader of U2, is one of the few personifications of the epic and legendary aspect of rock, The Edge is no less important, precisely because he has demonstrated over the years that his initial approach to guitar playing, which derived from the punk ethic (few notes, no virtuosity, little technical skill), was the right one to renovate rock and guitar playing from the bottom up. In the 1980s, when the electronic keyboard was dominant and it seemed that the electric guitar was doomed, The Edge was the musician who proved that there was still plenty of room left for the guitar, or better, that the guitar could become a totally new instrument.

And he was a natural foil for the theatrical and long-winded guitarists that dominated heavy metal and pop music in this period, remaining magnificently essential and splendidly creative – as can be seen in the latest productions of U2, which are largely based on the sound of his guitar. Very rarely doing solos, always playing in arpeggios, The Edge has renovated the style of rhythmic guitar playing, restoring the primary role it must have in every rock band worthy of the name.

Gibson Explorer
Gibson Les Paul Custom
Fender Stratocaster

< **The innovative use of delay** The Edge founded the U2 band along with Bono, Larry Mullen Jr., and Adam Clayton. His style is based on the innovative use of delay, which was a decisive factor in the creation of the Irish band's sound.

> **U2, 1983** U2 participating in the UK television program *The Tube*, in Newcastle in 1983. The arrival of U2 on the rock scene brought new wave music to a higher level of international popularity.

< Pop Mart Tour The Edge on stage in Las Vegas in 1997, during the first stage of the U2 band's Pop Mart Tour. In live performances the Irish guitarist creates extraordinary sounds, with a range of effects that he uses in a highly original manner.

> Tribute to America The poster of the 1988 film *Rattle and Hum*. Together with the double album of the same title, this movie was a great tribute that the Irish band wanted to pay to America and its music.

U2
RATTLE AND HUM
THE MOVIE

PG

Early morning, April 4
Shot rings out in the Memphis sky
Free at last, they took your life
They could not take your pride

In the name of love
What more in the name of love...
(1984 - Pride)

EDDIE VAN HALEN

Eddie Van Halen has always maintained that in theory guitars are built badly, because between every string there is an interval of a fourth, except for the G and B strings, which is a major third, which means that if you play an E chord in tune, an octave higher it will be slightly out of tune. This belief led to the guitar style of the Dutch musician who moved to the United States as a boy. In fact, the special tuning he used in order to avoid the problem of the interval of a major third often caused dissonances in his solos that became their most evident feature.

In many respects Van Halen, with his combination of virtuosity, innovation, and hedonism, embodied the commercial dimension of rock music in the 1980s: introspective, very technical, and withdrawn into itself.

He has become famous for his playing technique as well as for his inventions, which grew out of the need to adapt his instrument to his needs and which then became a style. As he himself stated, when he was listening to a solo by Jimmy Page in "Heartbreaker," he got the idea of using the index finger of his right hand as the fifth finger (beside the four fingers of the left hand) on the guitar neck, an idea that led to the "tapping" technique he developed to such a degree. This technique was actually already being adopted by guitarists such as Steve Hackett, Brian May, and Ace Frehley, but the drastic use Van Halen made of it was such that before the first Van Halen record came out Eddie always used to play his solos with his back to the audience so that no one could see how he produced those new sounds.

Sounds are another great obsession of his, so much so that it led him to modify his amplifiers, pedals, and guitars and to build them himself. His most famous guitar is the Frankenstrat, a sort of hybrid that resulted from Van Halen's attempt to combine the sound of a Gibson with the sensibility of a Fender.

The most telling portrait of Van Halen as a guitarist is the one of him in the video clip of "Jump," one of his band's greatest hits, when he mimes a solo while looking into the camera, with a smile and an air of haughtiness and flippancy that provides an exact image of his solos – theatrical, merry, vital, carefree, highly technical, and incurably empty.

< Hard rock and pop Eddie Van Halen playing his guitar during a concert given by Van Halen in 1984. In the mid-1980s, the band reached the peak of its popularity with an entertaining mixture of hard rock and pop.

> A Dutch American Van Halen in New York in 1984. The guitarist was born and grew up in Holland, but he took American citizenship in the 1960s, when his family moved to the United States.

Following pages

< > On stage, 1982 On stage, 1982 Three members of the Van Halen band – Michael Anthony, David Lee Roth, and Eddie Van Halen – in a photo taken during a 1982 concert. Eddie was one of the first guitarists to "customize" his instrument, modifying it according to his expressive needs.

(custom-built guitars)
Ernie Ball Music Man Van Van Halen

YNGWIE MALMSTEEN

< > **Metal guitar playing** Yngwie Malmsteen performs at the Brendan Byrne Arena in East Rutherford, New Jersey in September 1985. Malmsteen was one of the legends of metal guitar playing in the 1980s and 1990's.

Either you love him or you hate him. There is no middle path. Yet, with his stage presence and style, the Swedish guitarist Yngwie Malmsteen has been a decisive influence on the history and development of heavy metal, so much so that he is the only other guitarist in the world besides Eric Clapton to have a signature model in the Fender catalog, the Fender Malmsteen, which is a Stratocaster with a scalloped fingerboard. Those who admire him point out that his style is very personal, based on a variety of wide vibrato techniques, on aggressive and incisive picking, and on fast phrasing that is marked by very varied rhythm and rich melody.

Those who dislike him take into consideration his inconstant production, the excessive "baroque" effect of his solos, with the numerous useless trills he plays to embellish his already verbose style, and the use of speed to the detriment of any original idea. Despite all this, Malmsteen is one of the most popular and highly appreciated guitarists of the metal generation, capable of attracting large crowds to his live concerts, and who has achieved a long series of successes from the mid-1980s to the present.

On his website is the eye-catching phrase: "The day Jimi Hendrix died Malmsteen was born." In part, this phrase indicates the extraordinary impact Hendrix's music had on Malmsteen's personal life and musical career. Although most guitarists consider Jimi Hendrix an irreplaceable figure, a rock giant, a musical example to be followed, Yngwie Malmsteen's idol is instead, and most revealingly, the great 19th-century Italian violinist Niccolò Paganini, whose *24 Capricci* were the primary inspiration for the Swedish guitarist. When Malmsteen heard these pieces for the first time he decided he wanted to become a virtuoso, an innovator, the person who would explore a new field of music in which the electric guitar and rock music would be combined with virtuosity and classical music. His "neo-classical" style became famous in the 1980s, influencing such guitarists as Jason Becker, Paul Gilbert, Marty Friedman, Tony MacAlpine, and Vinnie Moore. And there is no doubt that, leaving aside personal taste, Malmsteen has helped to elevate the study of the rock guitar to a technical level and expressive complexity that were unknown in the 1980s. Irrespective of the quality of his music, it is no accident that Malmsteen has appeared in the annual ratings of the best guitarists in the world for over 20 years.

Fender Stratocaster

It will rip up your mind
And death you will find
Life is just a game
And death is just the same ...
(1983 - Now Your Ships Are Burned)

> **Lars Johan Yngve Lannerbäck** The Swede Yngwie Malmsteen (real name Lars Johan Yngve Lannerbäck) performing in New York City, 1988. He is one of the pioneers of the fusion of heavy metal and classical music.

MICK JONES

Decidedly more daring and idealistic than his nihilistic contemporaries, the Sex Pistols, but also more open to experimenting and even compromising by drawing on outside influences, Mick Jones was the personification of the Clash until the other members decided otherwise in 1983. They ousted him from the group and effectively ended the band's powerful sense of drive. As a pretext, they accused him of having betrayed the rough and spare spirit of punk in favor of a more elegant rock. And yet, during the band's six golden years, Jones and Joe Strummer had been the band's creative spirit. The aesthetic and the sound came mostly from Jones, having long since fallen for the idea of the rock star and enduring the most bitter disappointments and terrible humiliations in order to achieve recognition.

Dropped from his first band, the Delinquents, just before recording their first demo but still determined to achieve a breakthrough, Jones refused to give in and started all over again. What he had in mind at this point, though, was no longer a glam rock band like the previous one, but the creation of a sound that was angrier and more authentically rock and provocative. It was not by chance that the first name thought up for the band that was then to become the Clash, was London SS.

Jones had been inspired by the New York Dolls. The way this group moved on stage, their way of presenting themselves, and of interpreting their music had driven him to form a group that could compete with the newly emerging Sex Pistols. After hurriedly hiring himself a guitarist, a bass player, and a drummer (in the best get-a-move-on and don't-waste-time traditions of punk) and having found an ideally suitable singer in Joe Strummer, Mick Jones had everything he needed,

including a new name that would now never change.

However, it still required two albums (each a success) before reaching the perfection of "London Calling," a record in which punk and reggae took in many other influences (pop, rockabilly, hard rock, R&B ...) offering a brazen challenge to past musical heritage but still capable of combining pieces of such differing origin, all of which was to become the band's truly distinguishing characteristic. After the Clash came Big Audio Dynamite and then Carbon/Silicon. The mix of styles and sonorities are all contained in the sound and style of Jones' guitar, totally distant from that of his rock predecessors, essentially devoid of solo contributions and perfectly balanced between punk, rock, and reggae.

< > **Reggae and soul in punk rock** Joe
Strummer, the vocalist of the Clash, and Mick
Jones, their guitarist, performing at the
Paradiso in Amsterdam in 1978. Jones's guitar
style is a highly original mixture of reggae and
soul music that is grafted onto punk rock.

Gibson Les Paul

< **Social battles** A Rock Against Racism concert held at the Love Music Hate Racism carnival held in Victoria Park in 1978. The English band was always in the front line of the political and social battles of their country in the 1980s.

> **With the Clash in 1979** Mick Jones on stage with the Clash in 1979. After he left the group, Jones founded several other bands, such as Big Audio Dynamite and Carbon/Silicon.

RICHIE
SAMBORA

In the 1980s and 1990s, when the electric guitar had become almost obsolete because of the triumph first of the electronic keyboard and then of samplers and the world of DJs and rappers, among those musicians who were at the fore of the "resistance" was Richie Sambora, the Bon Jovi guitarist. As well as his exemplary technical prowess and background, Sambora also personified the decadence of rock in the most complete fashion, passing from the strong influence of metal in his early career to a form of pop rock that was apparently energetic and very polished. In any case, his sound, a light "translation" of the styles of hard rock and then rock blues, characterized all the band's successes, although he achieved his best results as a soloist in two albums *(Stranger in This Town and Undiscovered Truth)*, in which, no longer hampered by the commercial demands and needs of Bon Jovi, he gave vent to his personal passions, his love for rock blues and his sophisticated and complex compositional talent.

The metal roots of Sambora's approach to guitar playing are quite evident. But in a band that has made catchy tunes its trademark, he could not help adding a super-fast playing technique to the pop style. Awarded prizes for his lyrical solos and appealing riffs, Sambora is as much the driving force behind the success of Bon Jovi as Jon Bon Jovi himself.

Sambora, who plays two classic instruments, alternating a Les Paul with a Stracoaster, is quite receptive to the use of effects, which he utilizes to quite a degree in pieces that have become significant hits. For example, "Living on A Prayer" and "It's My Life" are filled with effects created by the talk box device. Proof of the fact that he and his band depend upon one another is the lack of success of his solo productions (two albums that came out in 1991 and 1998), while with Bob Jovi Sambora hugely influenced rock guitar playing in the 1980s and 1990s.

Gibson Les Paul
Fender Stratocaster

Made in America, nineteen fifty nine,
Born down by the factories, cross the Jersey City line.
Raised on radio, just a jukebox kid,
I was alright.
(1977 - Made in America)

> **In love with rock blues** Richie Sambora on stage in Texas in
1989. Gifted with exceptional technique, he is in love with rock
blues, and he often influences the direction of Bon Jovi, of which
he is one of the leading members, toward this music.

SLASH

Slash was the pop icon of the electric guitar, of hard rock, and of what the rock aesthetic became in the 1980s. Idolized as the lord of guitar playing at the height of his fame, and considered by many to be a musician gifted with extraordinary creativity, Slash has not managed to survive his myth, enjoying what in sum was a brief moment of popularity from the late 1980s to the early 1990s, after which he became a "luxury item" as a session musician, a guest guitarist, due to his extraordinary media clout. But over and above his success, Slash was certainly not a guitarist whose work was crucial to the evolution of rock guitar playing. On the contrary, he helped to "consolidate" rock guitar playing during the golden period of Guns N' Roses,

concentrating on spectacular showmanship, speed, and special effects to the detriment of originality.

In an interview with *Rolling Stone,* Slash declared that his "awakening" took place when he was 14 years old, while he was trying to seduce a girl in her home and was listening to music by Aerosmith: "It hit me like a ton of bricks. I sat there listening to it over and over, and totally blew off this girl. I remember riding my bike back to my grandma's house knowing that my life had changed. Now I identified with something."

Slash has had many famous collaborations, recording with

the likes of Alice Cooper, Eric Clapton, and on up to Ray Charles, Stevie Wonder, and James Stewart; the most memorable of all was the one with Michael Jackson, from *Dangerous* to *HIStory*. Proof of his status as a musical icon is his having been awarded a star in the Rock Walk Of Fame together with Jimmy Page and Eddie Van Halen "for the greatness of the musical phenomenon he has represented."

< **With Velvet Revolver, 2007** Slash, con i Velvet Revolver, suona sul palco della ventiduesima Rock'n'roll Hall of Fame Induction Ceremony, al Waldorf Astoria Hotel di New York, nel marzo del 2007.

Gibson Les Paul Custom
Gibson Flying V
Fender Stratocaster
Fender Telecaster

Welcome to the jungle / We've got fun 'n' games / We got everything

< The rebirth of hard rock Slash performing at Wembley in 1994. With his very special look, Slash brought about the "rebirth" of hard rock, together with Guns N' Roses, after the new wave period.

> A pop icon of the electric guitar Slash during a concert held at the Elserhalle, Munich in 2004. The Velvet Revolver band is the American "supergroup" with which Slash regained his popularity after his stint with Guns N' Roses.

you want / Honey, we know the names...   (1987 - Welcome to the Jungle)

MIKE McCREADY

Mike McCready exemplifies the combination of the violent and instinctive music of Santana and Hendrix with the smoother guitar style of Kiss or Aerosmith's Joe Perry. He plays intimate, improvised blues that aim at winning over the audience by speaking a language it can understand.

This is the reason why at first he was not considered one of the leading contemporary guitarists, despite the fact that he was one of the founding members of Pearl Jam who, after the release of the album *Ten* (1991), became rock legends. He was not considered a "guitar hero" because of his apparently modest, unassuming style, his simple approach, and his singular sound.

Paradoxically, an accident drew attention to his hidden qualities. During the recording of *Temple Of The Dog*, a group tribute conceived by Chris Cornell that merged members of Soundgarden and Pearl Jam to pay homage to Andrew Wood (the vocalist of Mother Love Bone), McCready was in the recording studio to cut "Reach Down" and, according to what the Soundgarden drummer Matt Cameron says, during the four-minute solo in the song his headphone monitors fell off and he had to play the rest of the solo without hearing anything but his own guitar. His amazing performance, played without backing track, was immortalized in the album of the same name that revealed McCready's true nature and skill.

An essential rock/pop soloist but a free and instinctive bluesman, McCready never plays the same solo twice; he changes it and improvises, with (as he himself says) Stevie Ray Vaughan in mind, but also directly or indirectly inspired by less virtuoso guitarists such as Pete Townshend of The Who. It was precisely this minimalist yet intense style advocated by McCready that contributed to the slow change in the 1990s in which rock guitar playing passed from the indulgent excesses of the preceding years to the quest for fewer notes that were also the right ones. McCready, even more than Kurt Cobain, personifies the essence of grunge, its determination to emancipate rock from the abysmal commercialism that reigned in the United States in the 1980s, when this genre either became more and more like pop or withdrew into the shell of heavy metal.

McCready believes in the sound of the guitar and makes it the linchpin of the music produced by Pearl Jam, the instrument that can still unleash emotions, but without succumbing to the temptation of theatrical, spectacular showmanship, and without the need to parade a particular technique. With his spare and essential style, McCready is unrestrained above all in live performances, where he becomes the passionate electric motor of Pearl Jam.

**A confidence man, but why so beleagued?
Hes not a leader, hes a texas leaguer
Swinging for the fence, got lucky with a strike
Drilling for fear, makes the job simple
Born on third, thinks he got a triple**

(2002 - Bushleaguer)

> **Los Angeles, 2008** Mike McCready of Pearl Jam in a concert held in 2008 in Los Angeles, during the celebration dedicated to The Who organized by VH1. McCready is one of the best guitarists of his generation.

KURT COBAIN

Whether he deserves it or not, Kurt Cobain (1967–94) has undeniably become a legend somewhat in the vein of Jimi Hendrix, Janis Joplin, or Jim Morrison. Despite the fact that he did not share the revolutionary ideas that became the vogue in the late 1960s, because he had a different approach to both life and music, his style and the success of Nirvana, together with his suicide, ensured him a place among the Olympians of guitar playing.

The way his music, as performed at Nirvana's concerts, merged rock, metal, and pop melodies and characterized by a disappointment with life and his personal relationships, most certainly had a great impact on the music of the 1990s and on all American grunge and alternative rock on the Seattle scene. At this point mention must be made of the psychotropic drugs Cobain was forced to take at an early age to control his hyperactive nature, as well as his being abandoned by his parents, events that, together with his untimely death, were major factors in creating his legendary fame. The most important, famous, and influential musician of depressed rock died at the height of his success by shooting himself.

From a purely musical standpoint, on the other hand, as a guitarist Cobain was certainly not gifted with brilliant technique, but he skillfully merged two distinct aspects of modern rock music. *Nevermind* is one of the most important albums released in the 1990s, with its powerful, violent music that succeeds in communicating over and above the lyrics (which are often very difficult to understand because of the poor pronunciation). Then there is the unplugged concert for MTV, which was later released as an album, that shows how, even when all the "dirty" sound, distortion, and effects are cleaned up, Kurt Cobain's songs are really great in the true sense of the word. In both these cases what dominates the Nirvana sound is his guitar, which he plays with no frills, hyper-amplified, and dirty – a style that has had a great influence on an entire generation of guitarists who arrived on the scene after him.

Fender Mustang
Fender Telecaster
Fender Stratrocaster

‹ › **An unplugged concert for MTV** Kurt
Cobain in the Hilversum Studios in Holland,
playing an acoustic guitar. The "unplugged"
concert that Nirvana recorded for MTV is one
of the high points of their musical production.

With the lights out its less dangerous
Here we are now
Entertain us
I feel stupid and contagious
Here we are now
Entertain us
(1991 - Smells Like Teen Spirit)

Kurt Cobain
Nirvana

"I always wanted to try the experience of street life, seeing how boring my adolescent life was in Aberdeen, but I was never independent enough to do it. I waited in line for meal tickets and I lived under a bridge. In the end I moved to Olympia."
(Kurt Donald Cobain)

> **New York, 1993** Kurt Cobain with a Fender Mustang guitar in a live performance with Nirvana in New York
City in 1993. His style was an essential part of grunge rock for many of the guitarists who followed him.

LENNY KRAVITZ

Lenny Kravitz has spent more than 20 years playing rock, and after a long period as a cult artist marked by consistently positive reviews and acclaim and by the great interest shown by audiences, in the new millennium he has also enjoyed great success and has risen in the charts in many countries of the world. This success was well deserved, because the American guitarist, vocalist, and composer has succeeded in constructing a symbolic bridge between the roots of rock in the 1960s and wholly modern sensibility and taste. But is Lenny Kravitz really interested in reviving the past? "I don't know, I don't think so", Kravitz said, adding: "I don't analyze music in this way and I don't like labels. I love music, all music, and I'm not afraid to use sounds or atmospheres that I like, from both classical and psychedelic or soul." This is certainly true: his songs have a spirit that is difficult to ascribe to only one style.

They can be rock songs that are often both pulsating and rhythmic, acid yet subtle funk, ballads both rugged and romantic. But his unmistakable sound can undoubtedly be pigeonholed – it is supremely 1960s, incorporating a host of "vintage" instruments such as valve amplifiers and analog technology. Mr. Kravitz does not like electronics and by no means does he want people to see – even by mistake – any affinity with the music of today: "It sounds all the same, the bands vie with one another to produce the same sound, there's no room for an artist to express what he really is," he says with conviction. His sincerity is amply demonstrated by his music with easily recognizable echoes of Hendrix and Sly Stone, and songs that combine different sentiments and references. First and foremost, there is rock, supported by sure-handed and sharp electric guitar playing, but there is also funk and reggae, love songs and soul music. Kravitz can do everything; he sings, plays the bass, drums, and keyboards. But his musical universe revolves above all around the guitar, which he plays with masterful technique, merging elements of blues and rock with remarkable creative talent. "Music is my life," Kravitz says, "and the guitar is the instrument that allows me to live it." What more could one ask?

< A multi-instrumentalist Kravitz performing in 1995 in Charleston, South Carolina. He is a composer and multi-instrumentalist; besides the guitar, he plays bass, piano, drums, harmonica, and sitar.

> From the Beatles to Led Zeppelin Lenny Kravitz is at his ease with the most classic rock style, marked by such influences as the Beatles as well as Led Zeppelin. He was married to the actress Lisa Bonet, and they have a daughter.

Gibson ES175
Fender Stratocaster

< **New Orleans, 2002** Lenny Kravitz performing at the New Orleans Jazz Festival of 2002. He is one of the most interesting and versatile musicians of his generation, with an extremely essential and expressive style.

> **1960s and 1970s sounds** Lenny Kravitz on stage at the Boston Fleet Center in 2004. In his live performances the American musician offers a splendid mixture of 1960s and 1970s sounds, which he updates with modern sensibility.

TRENT REZNOR

Trent Reznor had nobody to play with or, perhaps we should say, nobody that satisfied him, nobody with whom to share a few spare moments to devote to music, and so he decided to do everything by himself.

It was the end of the 1980s and Reznor was working for the recording studios Right Track, whose equipment he used to use in his own time to create music under the alias Nine Inch Nails. His idea was to copy Prince in playing all the instruments by himself and in this way reach the desired sound. Nine Inch Nails was always essentially Reznor, with some added members only for the tours or occasional recording sessions.

The 1990s saw him as a very active protagonist in the cultural life of the musical world. As Nine Inch Nails he not only contributed, and in a considerable way, to the launch of the era of industrial rock, but he also lent his support to many other equally important and influential projects, such as the albums of Marilyn Manson.

Reznor's is the story of a pure outsider from the provinces, growing up surrounded by mythical figures (from the worlds of television, radio, and the press) knowing that he could never reach their level, exactly as he explained in the 1994 album *The Downward Spiral*. His childhood could not be called unhappy, rather just "protected" in the most claustrophobic and limiting sense of the word. Because of this he, too, became a spokesman during the depressed mood of the punk age for discontent and youthful depression.

He attracted a huge number of followers or "generic imitations," as he liked to call them, and the impact of his records was a determining factor on the music of the 1990s and acknowledged as such by the greater part of the musical world. David Bowie himself, who wanted to tour with him in 1995, compared his impact to that of the Velvet Underground in terms of the influence exercised in his era.

i am the voice inside your head and i control you
i am the lover in your bed and i control you
i am the sex that you provide and i control you
i am the hate you try to hide and i control you
(1994 - Mr. Self Destruct)

JOHN FRUSCIANTE

John Frusciante is one of the few to realize the dream of all musicians by becoming a member of the band that he particularly adored. His journey from the auditorium to being on stage with the Red Hot Chili Peppers took place when the Los Angeles group was still a local band that performed in small nightclubs, and whose main feature was that "the audience feels no different from the band at all," as Frusciante himself said. It was this that allowed him to become acquainted with the members of the band (at first the bass player Flea) and then make an audition after the death of the Peppers' guitarist Hillel Slovack, from whom Frusciante had learned guitar playing and whom he greatly admired.

Above all it was the desire to become part of the world of "sex, drugs, and rock and roll" that drove him to the Red Hot Chili Peppers. In fact, Frusciante had abandoned the tryouts to become part of Zappa's musical family when he found out that Frank prohibited drug use among his band members. However, his early experience with the Red Hot Chili Peppers was limited to two albums, *Mother's Milk* (1989) and *Blood Sugar Sex Magik* (1991). His contribution was a major factor in the success of both albums. His style, on the borderline between funk and punk and ably combining hard rock and psychedelic music, helped to create the unique sound and style of the California band.

After recording *Blood Sex Sugar Magik* the fame of the Red Hot Chili Peppers grew enormously and Frusciante could not cope with the frenzied tide of events that followed. Drug abuse, excesses, and even a vision of the world that caused him to believe that Peppers was a small rock band that had to content itself with success in local club gigs rather than on the international scene, all led him to suddenly abandon the group right in the middle of a world tour. Thus began a period as a soloist in which he became dangerously dependent on heroin and also made two albums, *Niandra Lades and Usually Just a T-Shirt,* which came out in 1995, and *Smile from the Streets You Hold* (1997), that were not especially successful in this long period of crisis, a crisis he managed to emerge from with great difficulty five years later, ready to rejoin the Peppers.

Since then, not only has the band enjoyed growing success, but Frusciante has regained his former creativity and energy, recording the solo album *To Record Only Water for Ten Days* in 2001, a huge work consisting of six compact discs titled *Ataxia* in 2004 and, in 2007, its sequel, *Ataxia II.*

Frusciante's style derives from the punk aesthetic: few solos, strong rhythm, hard and full sounds, all mixed with funk sensibility, which in a short time became the trademark of the California band's style and sound.

< **Funk, rap and rock** Red Hot Chili Peppers during a 2002 concert in Rotterdam. This American band is one of the most popular on the contemporary rock scene, with its extraordinary combination of funk, rap, and rock.

> **Las Vegas, 2005** John Frusciante with Red Hot Chili Peppers in a Las Vegas concert held in 2005. Frusciante became a member of the California band after the death of its first lead guitarist, Hillel Slovak.

TOM MORELLO

Undoubtedly, the most up-to-date point of reference for young guitarists who want to explore different, modern universes of sound is the guitarist of Audioslave, which was formed by the remaining members of Rage Against the Machine, who were among the authors of true crossover in rock music. This band, one of the few that succeeded in felicitously merging metal funk and rap, and that conquered the public partly thanks to video clips, distinguishes itself for the political commitment and activity that Tom Morello has encouraged in the band (often his baseball caps also bear a political message).

Clearly he is so competent and versatile because he assimilated, profited from, and then sublimated the influence and teaching of both Jimmy Page and Van Halen, and has consequently made a crucial contribution to riffs, solo playing, and accompaniment, as well as to the creation of sounds and effects that are the distinguishing feature of Rage Against the Machine.

Morello is a disc jockey of the guitar. Like Jimi Hendrix, his mastery of the instrument has allowed him to do anything he wants with it and to play in a wholly unorthodox fashion (tapping the strings of the guitar with his jack cable, for example). An adept at obtaining a variety of sounds from his instrument, Morello uses many different guitars, from the Telecaster to Les Paul and Ibanez, tuning the last-mentioned in a different manner (mainly in E and D).

The essence of his style, the fusion of funk and rock, has made him one of the leading innovators of contemporary guitar playing, alongside Frusciante of the Red Hot Chili Peppers band, which has paved the way for a generation of instrumentalists who no longer feel the need when playing rock to adhere to the canons of blues and prefer to move more freely into more modern areas of music-making. What is even more important, Morello has updated the vocabulary of his instrument, which he has offered to the generation that grew up with electronic keyboards and samplers and that obviously demanded more from the guitar than preceding generations had done. Morello is one of the most ingenious, entertaining, energetic, and original musicians that rock music has produced in the last two decades. He is a guitarist gifted with great technique and expression.

Mongrel Custom "Arm the Homeless"
Fender Custom Stratocaster "Soul Power"
Fender Telecaster "Sendero Luminoso"

< **Rage Against The Machine, 2007** Tom Morello, the guitarist of Rage Against the Machine playing live during the New York stage of the band's Rock the Bells tour at Randall's Island in July 2007.

> **Rock, metal and funk** Morello's style incorporates elements of rock, metal, and funk in an extremely original combination that has strongly influenced the style of Rage Against the Machine.

KIRK HAMMETT

Dave Mustaine was the original guitar soloist of the Metallica band, but so much violence on his part was too much even for his metal colleagues, and in 1983 the band was forced to replace him with another guitarist who was already a part of the metal music world with his band Exodus and a pupil of Joe Satriani. During the series of auditions, this young guitarist distinguished himself and stunned the other members of Metallica with his close resemblance to European rockers (who at the time were idolized), such as Ritchie Blackmore.

However, in order to judge the incredible impact Kirk Hammet had on Metallica, you must not listen to the first album he cut with them, *Kill 'Em All,* because many of the guitar parts had already been written by Mustaine, and out of respect the newcomer played them as written. Only afterwards did his personal style emerge. So, if *Master of Puppets* is considered one of the most important albums in the history of heavy metal, it is due in large part to the fundamental contribution made by Kirk Hammett, the new member of Metallica who became the driving force behind the band's sound.

Undoubtedly, the most obvious element of his style is the exaggerated, programmatic, and "baroque" use of the wah-wah pedal, which Hammett himself considers "an extension of my personality." "They'll have to cut off my leg if they want me to stop me from using the wah-wah pedal." But there are also other, much more delicate elements in his style that are on an equal footing with the continuous references to Hendrix, which with time have become increasingly evident, to the point of being explicit quotations in his live performance solos.

Certainly, at this stage he was no longer the thrash metal guitarist who attracted the attention of Metallica. A transition had begun, the same one that in the late 1990s led the entire band (especially Hammett) to revise their image, totally abandoning what had always been their heavy metal look (long hair, T-shirts, studs, leather jackets, etc.) and acquiring a much more sober and cosmopolitan look that had only some references to metal culture.

Hammett's style is monumental, based to quite a degree on the use of volume and the potential of resonance as part of an overall, exaggerated amplification, in keeping with the rules of this musical genre. But there are also more refined notes, arpeggios and ballads, a palette of colors that this fine guitarist is not afraid to utilize, especially in order to broaden the expressive range of his style and, more generally speaking, of the California band, a style that he was the first to forge and, as time passed by, to innovate, with the aim of breaking free as much as possible from the clichés of the genre and of never remaining shut up within the confines of a mammoth and often awkward and cumbersome sound.

ESP KH-2
ESP M-II "Boris Karloff Mummy"

< **The trash metal legend** Kirk Hammett
on stage with Metallica in 2003. Hammett
replaced Dave Mustaine in the band and
soon became a legend of trash metal and
one of the most highly appreciated
guitarists in the world.

> **The move toward hard rock** Metallica
on stage during the 2003 Roskilde
Festival with guitarist Kirk Hammett.
In the 1990s Hammett led the California
band toward a hard rock style.

So close, no matter how far
Couldn't be much more from the heart
Forever trusting who we are
No, nothing else matters
(2000 - Nothing Else Matters)

< **Amid the flames** It was March 20, 2004 when Kirk Hammett was immortalized in this photograph, surrounded by flames during a concert that Metallica held at Boise State University, Idaho.

> **California, 2004** Kirk Hammett playing with Metallica in the final stage of their 2004 Madly in Anger with the World tour, in San Jose, Calfornia. Hammett was classified in 11th place among the best guitarists in the world by *Rolling Stone*.

BEN HARPER

Ben Harper is one of the few singers and songwriters of our time who does not make us regret the past. Since the mid-1990s he has been the torchbearer of a difficult but effective formula that combines the topicality of young rock with the social commitment of blues songs. One notes this from his first album, *Welcome to The Cruel World* (1994), all the way to the last one, the much discussed *Lifeline* (2007). And yet, despite that fact that he is world famous as a singer and composer, Harper is also an excellent guitarist.

Harper is gifted with a highly sophisticated technique that is never exaggerated. Muddy Waters is certainly one of his inspirations, and in fact Harper is at his best when he uses the acoustic guitar. A specialist of the slide guitar, he is among the very few, together with Clapton and Hendrix, who is able to forge a perfect match between the singing and its accompaniment.

The bottleneck, a metal tube placed over the finger like a thimble that slides over the strings, certainly was not used for the first time by Harper (in fact, it began with David Evans), but by taking it from a pop repertory and with the help of video clips, he made it a household word even among a public not versed in guitar techniques and technology. We could consider Harper one of the "minor" heroes of modern rock blues guitar playing, a field with so many good performers that his talent, like that of equally gifted guitarists such as Jon Butler, often goes unacknowledged. That is to say, while it is true that Harper has been extremely successful as a singer and

songwriter, he deserves more acclaim as a guitarist as well for his dry and essential sound, his complete expressive range, and for his utter disregard of useless virtuosity despite his great technique.

However, although he is not a "guitar hero," Ben Harper is one of the most highly esteemed singer-guitarists today, and he is not even forty years old. Indeed, with a luthier grandfather and grandmother and mother who are guitarists, this could not have been otherwise.

< > **A personal style** An extraordinary vocalist and guitarist, Ben Harper is master of practically all the musical genres – folk, rock, blues, gospel, reggae, and soul – with a highly personal and passionate style. Furthermore, he is one of the best slide guitarists around.

Index

> Photo Credits

Richard E. Aaron/Redferns/Getty Images: pages 120, 164, 175

Stephen Albanese/Michael Ochs Archive/Getty Images: pages 338-339

AP/LaPresse: pages 192, 213, 320

Steve Appleford/Corbis: page 229

Don Arnold/WireImage/Getty Images: page 221

Howard Barlow/Redferns/Getty Images: page 232

Dick Barnatt/Redferns/Getty Images: pages 150-151, 151

Catherine Bauknight/ZUMA/LaPresse: page 314

Roberta Bayley/Redferns/Getty Images: pages 234-235

Paul Bergen/Redferns/Getty Images: pages 267, 272, 273, 324, 327

Bettman/Corbis: pages 88

Gene Blevins/Corbis: pages 38-39

Chris Butler/Zuma/LaPresse: page 334

Henrietta Butler/Redferns/Getty Images: page 125

Sandy Caspers/Redferns/Getty Images: page 259

Elio Castoria/epa/Corbis: page 159

Nobby Clark/Hulton Archive/Getty Images: page 79

Corbis: pages 225, 289

Lester Cohen/WireImage/Getty Images: page 181

David Corio/Redferns/Getty Images: pages 153

David Corio/Michael Ochs Archives/Getty Images: pages 231, 233

Fin Costello/Redferns/Getty Images: pages 143, 144-145, 147, 171, 182-183, 197, 201, 226, 261, 275

Christie's Images Ltd: pages 107, 111

Pete Cronon/Redferns/Getty Images: page 178 right

James Cumpsty/Redferns/Getty Images: page 255

Grant Davies/Redferns/Getty Images: pages 184, 185

Alessandro Della Bella/epa/Corbis: page 203

Ian Dickson/Redferns/Getty Images: pages 146, 169, 195, 198-199, 323

Henry Diltz/Corbis: pages 65, 128, 205, 206

Debi Doss/Hulton Archive/Getty Images: pages 167, 168

Rico D'Rozario/Redferns/Getty Images: page 238

Erica Echenberg/Redferns/Getty Images: pages 152, 269

Echoes Archives/Redferns/Getty Images: page 31

Brigitte Engl/Redferns/Getty Images: pages 262-263

Everett Collection/Contrasto: pages 29, 42, 89

David Farrell/Redferns/Getty Images: page 86

Deborah Feingold/Corbis: page 254

Rick Friedman/Corbis: page 317

Colin Fuller/Redferns/Getty Images: page 163

GAB Archives/Redferns/Getty Images: pages 26 right, 33, 105, 136, 271

Charlie Gillett Archive/Redferns/Getty Images: page 173

Mick Gold/Redferns/Getty Images: pag: 73

Harry Goodwin/Redferns/Getty Images: page 54

Scott Gries/Getty Images: page 298

Bryan Haraway/Getty Images: page 325

Dave Hogan/Getty Images: page 71

Mick Hutson/Redferns/Getty Images: pages 241, 256-257, 300, 307

JazzSign/Lebrecht Music & Art/Corbis: page 37

Steve Jennings/WireImage/Getty Images: page 337

Jason Kempin/FilMagic/Getty Images: page 328

Keystone Features/Hulton Archive/Getty Images: page 126

Bob King/Redferns/Getty Images: page 149

K&K ULF KRUGER OHG/Redferns/Getty Images: page 87

Robert Knight/Redferns/Getty Images: pages 98, 100-101

Kim Komenich/Time Life Pictures/Getty Images: page 44

Brooks Kraft/Sygma/Corbis: page 219

Jeff Kravitz/FilmMagic/Getty Images: page 305

Michel Linssen/Redferns/Getty Images: pages 82, 308, 309

John Livzey/Redferns/Getty Images: page 177

Bruno Marzi: pages 179

Jeffrey Mayer/pictorialpress.com: page 161

Jeffrey Mayer/WireImage/Getty Images: page 95

Kevin Mazur/WireImage/Getty Images: pages 186-187

Metronome/Getty Images: page 27

MJ Kim/Getty Images: page 77

Frank Micelotta/Getty Images: page 292

Ethan Miller/Getty Images: page 329

Gary Miller/WireImage/Getty Images: page 331

Chris Morphet/Redferns/Getty Images: pages 135, 138

Leon Morris/Redferns/Getty Images: page 316

Tim Mosenfelder/Corbis: pages 223, 335

Tim Mosenfelder/Getty Images: page 61

Bernd Muller/Redferns/Getty Images: page 333

Ilpo Musto: page 293

Ilpo Musto/Redferns/Getty Images: page 237

Paul Natkin/WireImage/Getty Images: pages 253, 265

New Eyes/Redferns/Getty Images: pages 154-155

Petra Niemeier/Redferns/Getty Images: page 109

Odile Noel/Lebrecht Music & Art/Contrasto: page 35

Michael Ochs Archives/Corbis: page 137

Michael Ochs Archives/Getty Images: pages 32, 36, 48, 57, 60, 90, 93, 97, 104, 108, 113, 165

Peter Pakvis/Redferns/Getty Images: page 332

Ed Perlstein/Redferns/Getty Images: page 11

Jan Persson/Redferns/Getty Images: pages 43 bottom, 45, 47, 55, 75, 103, 174, 189

Gilles Petard Collection/Redferns/Getty Images: page 30

Gesine Petter/Fotex: page 250

Photofest/Lebrecht Music & Art/Contrasto: page 117

Pictorial Press Ltd/Alamy: page 133

Stefan M. Prager/Redferns/Getty Images: page 301

Neal Preston/Corbis: pages 66-67, 81, 91, 121, 123, 130-131, 157, 158, 160, 191, 193 right, 211, 215, 216-217, 218, 239, 276, 278-279, 285, 291, 295, 297, 302, 319, 321

Andrew Putler/Redferns/Getty Images: page 140

Christina Radish/Redferns/Getty Images: page 313

Redferns/Getty Images: pages 246, 247

RB/Redferns/Getty Images: page 74

David Redferns/Redferns/Getty Images: page 129

Lorne Resnick/Redferns/Getty Images: page 193 left

Roger Ressmeyer/Corbis: pages 53, 63

Simon Ritter/Redferns/Getty Images: pages 260, 315

Ebet Roberts/Redferns/Getty Images: pages 9, 176, 222, 227, 245, 249, 251, 277, 280-281, 283, 311

John Rogers/Redferns/Getty Images: page 96

George Rose/Getty Images: page 43 top

Max Scheler/Redferns/Getty Images: page 85

Diana Scrimgeour/Redferns/Getty Images: page 70

Jon Sievert/Michael Ochs Archives/Getty Images: pages 51, 99, 178 left

Christopher Simon Sykes/Hulton Archive/Getty Images: page 127

Homer Sykes/Corbis: pages 68-69

Gai Terrell/Redferns/Getty Images: page 208

Time Life Pictures/Getty Images: page 80

Allan Titmuss/ARENA IMAGES/TopFoto.co.uk/Icponline: page 58

Lex Van Rossen/Redferns/Getty Images: pages 286-287

Rob Verhorst/Redferns/Getty Images: pages 119, 270

Roger Viollet/Archivi Alinari, Firenze: page 41

Chris Walter/WireImage/Getty Images: page 115, 207

Speke Watson/ARENA IMAGES/TopFoto.co.uk/Icponline: page 268

Val Wilmer/Redferns/Getty Images: page 288

Graham Wiltshire/Redferns/Getty Images: page 141

Gary Wolstenholme/Redferns/Getty Images: pages 242-243

Charlyn Zlotnik/Michael Ochs Archive/Getty Images: page 214

Per gentile concesione di Patrick Cusse & Christie Goodwin/CCPHOTOART.biz: page 7

Per gentile concessione di Gibson: pag, 26 left, 106

ERNESTO ASSANTE was born in 1958 and is a journalist and music critic for the Italian daily newspaper La Repubblica. In over 30 years in this field he has written articles for numerous weekly and monthly periodicals, both in Italy and abroad, including Epoca, L'Espresso, and Rolling Stone. He has also been active as a host for private radio stations and for Rai, the Italian state radio, and has also written for television. Assante has published several books on music: Bob Marley (Lato Side, 1980) Reggae (Savelli, 1981) The History of Rock (5 vols., Savelli, 1983) Rock and Other Stories (Arcana, 1984) Metropolitan Landscape (Feltrinelli, 1985)   The Journey of Black Music (Marcon, 1991) Genesis (Castelvecchi, 1997) Recorded Music (Audino, 2005) 33 Records You Can't Do Without (Einaudi, 2007) Rock Legends (White Star, 2008).

The Publisher would like to thank

Mogar Music S.p.A. , specially Giorgio Paganini
Gibson Italia, specially Eleonora Dal Pozzo
M. Casale Bauer S.p.a., specially Patrizia Masetti and Vilma Coltelli
Marco De Fabianis Manferto
Mick Brigden
Wendy Hoffhine

Special thanks are due to the following persons for their valuable collaboration
Joe Satriani
Adrian Belew

WHITE STAR PUBLISHERS

WS White Star Publishers® is a registered trademark
property of Edizioni White Star s.r.l.

© 2009 Edizioni White Star s.r.l.
Via Candido Sassone, 24
13100 Vercelli, Italy
www.whitestar.it

Translation by Richard Pierce
Editing by Sam Merrell

ISBN 978-88-544-0423-6
2 3 4 5 6   14 13 12 11 10

Printed in Indonesia

Rory **Gallagher**
Steve **Hackett**
Alex **Lifeson**
Steve **Morse**
Robbie **Krieger**
Johnny **Winter**
Steve **Howe**
Bruce **Springsteen**
Joe **Satriani**
Andy **Summers**
Johnny **Ramone**
Prince
Dave **Mustaine**
Michael **Schenker**
George **Thorogood**
Adrian **Belew**
Mark **Knopfler**
Steve **Vai**
Stevie Ray **Vaughan**
The **Edge**
Eddie **Van Halen**
Yngwie **Malmsteen**
Mick **Jones**
Richie **Sambora**
Slash
Mike **McCready**
Kurt **Cobain**
Lenny **Kravitz**
Trent **Reznor**
John **Frusciante**
Tom **Morello**
Kirk **Hammett**
Ben **Harper**